The Illusion of Inclusion

The Illusion of Inclusion

Global Inclusion, Unconscious Bias and the Bottom Line

Helen Turnbull, PhD, CSP

BUSINESS EXPERT PRESS

The Illusion of Inclusion: Global Inclusion, Unconscious Bias and the Bottom Line

Copyright © Business Expert Press, LLC, 2016.

First published in 2016 by
Business Expert Press, LLC
222 East 46th Street, New York, NY 10017
www.businessexpertpress.com

ISBN-13: 978-1-63157-457-3 (paperback)
ISBN-13: 978-1-63157-458-0 (e-book)

Business Expert Press Human Resource Management and Organizational Behavior Collection

Collection ISSN: 1946-5637 (print)
Collection ISSN: 1946-5645 (electronic)

Cover and interior design by Exeter Premedia Services Private Ltd., Chennai, India

First edition: 2016

10 9 8 7 6 5 4 3 2 1

Printed in the United States of America.

Abstract

We may say we want to be inclusive, but what if we really don't? What if our brains are hard-wired for selfishness and similarity and not for diversity and altruism? What if our vision of ourselves as well-intentioned people is at odds with the reality of who we really are and what we really think?

Having a diverse workforce is no guarantee that the work environment is inclusive and engaged. Companies hire for diversity and manage for similarity. We hire people for their difference and then teach them directly and indirectly what they have to do to fit in to the corporate culture. The 2015 Gallop Poll found that 51 percent of employees surveyed are "disengaged" at work and 17.2 percent are described as "actively disengaged."

The Illusion of Inclusion exposes a myriad of diverse reasons why people are not more fully engaged and directly addresses the need to own the unconscious biases and blind spots that are barriers to inclusion and offers you the key to unlock the "Geometry of Inclusion."

The *Illusion of Inclusion* takes the lid off Pandora's box and explores the complexity of inclusion; where affinity bias or "mini-me" syndrome and the need to fit in are unconsciously blocking our ability to be inclusive. The *Illusion of Inclusion* offers a road map through this complexity and an easy to comprehend model on how to minimize the impact of unconscious and conscious biases in order to leverage and retain top talent and embed an inclusive organizational culture.

Keywords

affinity bias, assimilation, covering, diversity, global inclusion, inclusion, unconscious bias

Contents

Testimonials

Dr. Helen Turnbull, has been in the Diversity field for over 28 years and is one of the most accomplished diversity professionals I know. She has contributed consequential assessment tools to the industry on unconscious bias and inclusion skills, and has been very involved with the globalization of the work in the field. It comes as no surprise that she would take the time to contribute this important work on Inclusion to the body of Diversity and Inclusion literature.

In this book, Helen tackles the reality of diversity paradoxes and acknowledges that in many organizations we may hire for diversity but manage for similarities. She encourages the reader to resist that temptation by staying focused on the benefits derived from valuing diversity. Dr. Turnbull also acknowledges that although valuing diversity is beneficial for organizations it can be very difficult to find the mutuality of purpose and respect necessary to move beyond the illusion and into inclusion. To that end, she provides the reader with some meaningful approaches to becoming more inclusive.

I strongly recommend this book for any Diversity and Inclusion professional or senior leader interested in making sustainable change within an organization.

—Ralph De Chabert, Chief Diversity Officer, Brown-Forman

If you've ever been confused by what "diversity" means or how to incorporate it, join the club, and instead learn about Helen Turnbull's seminal work on inclusion and how that's a different ballgame played in a different ballpark with much more intelligent rules.

—Alan Weiss, PhD, author, *Million Dollar Consulting,*
Million Dollar Maverick and over 60 other books

Acknowledgments

Every book I have ever read starts with Acknowledgments. I have always assumed that whoever the author was thanking were people who contributed in a meaningful way to the final product. However, it is only when you have walked a mile in those shoes that you really understand how much.

This book has been on my "I promise I will get it done one day" list for quite a few years. It is now finally a reality. There are many people, both personal and professional, who have contributed to my ongoing journey with inclusion. The people to whom I owe a deep and profound debt of gratitude are Alison Pullman for her willingness to read everything I wrote and provide feedback; Alan Weiss for encouraging me to finish the book proposal and helping me find an Agent and Publisher; and Barry Banther for introducing me to Chris Benguhe, my developmental editor. Chris I cannot thank you enough for your expert guidance and counsel. You are a master craftsman and a delight to work with. Your depth of knowledge in the writing process, sage advice, professionalism, and ongoing feedback have proved invaluable.

Introduction

From Human Nature to the Nature of Inclusion

What is the big deal about inclusion? It is easy to include others. All you have to do is make sure you actually notice people, smile, acknowledge them, say hello, make them feel good, include them in your conversation, seek their opinion, reassure them you like them, actively demonstrate you are listening, and help them feel validated and reassure them their ideas have value. Oh, is that all? This is beginning to sound challenging.

If you are like me, perhaps with some people in your life you can check every "inclusion" box, but there are others in your peripheral vision you simply don't see; some you choose not to see and some you do not want to see, or even wish didn't exist.

It is easy to be inclusive if I agree with you, or more importantly, if you agree with me. It is easy to be inclusive if I have some affinity for you. It is also easy to be inclusive if I need something from you, or if you need something from me that I am willing to share. As well-intentioned people, we believe we are inclusive of others and would conceptually support the idea of becoming more inclusive. Yet, evidence abounds we are better at excluding than including others. In short, the desire to be included and resistance to it are part of human nature. It does not come naturally to include everyone. Conversely, the desire to belong hauntingly follows us around like Peter Pan's lost shadow.

So let's admit it, being human really means being inclusive is full of caveats and conditions. We love it and we hate it; we crave it and we spurn it. I want to be included most of the time, but I don't always want to be inclusive. It is an intrinsic part of our human nature to be selective about who we include and how we choose to be included. Therein lies part of the diversity and inclusion challenge.

It's in Our DNA

Over the years of working in the field of Global Inclusion, Diversity, and Unconscious Bias, I have noticed an interesting phenomenon. We have a halo and horns blind spot when it comes to judging ourselves and others. When I ask people to vote anonymously via live polling during a keynote or workshop if their leaders create an inclusive environment, the results typically look like this (Figure I.1).

When I ask the same people about their *personal* contribution to creating an inclusive environment, the results typically look like this (Figure I.2).

The halo effect or bias blind spot always comes into play as we all think we are doing better than everyone else at being inclusive. That is our first blind spot. We also apply the horns effect to others as we typically believe our leaders are not doing as well as we think they should be.

If we believe it is other people and not ourselves, we will always be waiting for others to see the light, while not seeing the impact of our own unconscious biases and shortcomings. Catching our propensity for affinity bias, controlling our ego needs, admitting our resistance to change, and managing our own blind spots are all part of the journey. No one gets to be a phenomenological exception, including me. Regardless of your role in the organization, or your diversity, we all own a piece of the story. It is in our DNA.

[handwritten margin notes: Awareness and Phenomenon, distinct from existence]

Figure I.1 Perception of leadership contribution to inclusive culture

Source: Human Facets keynote findings (2015).

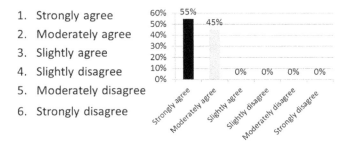

Figure I.2 Perception of individual contribution to inclusion

Source: Human Facets keynote findings (2015).

Where It All Began

My fascination with inclusion began, or so I thought, in 1985 when I was attending a workshop in Bethel, Maine, and was first introduced to the reality that people were excluded and treated differently based on their race, culture, gender, and/or sexual orientation. I vividly recall the first day when at a workshop a participant introduced herself as "I am Jacqui and I am a lesbian." I was stunned. I never heard anyone introduce themselves as a lesbian. I was not even sure then if I had ever consciously met a lesbian or heard people talk about lesbians. I was not even sure if we had lesbians in Scotland. My discomfort with this introduction caused me to walk cautiously around Jacqui for most of the program as I was not sure how to deal with my own naivety and discomfort. It was clearly my loss and at the same time a lesson learned. The shock was like a firecracker on July 4th, a jaw-dropping, eye popping, "are you kidding me" experience that made me ask myself "Where have I been most of my life?"

How is it possible I did not know these different points of view existed? What Kool-Aid was I drinking to miss such an important piece of the story? Did this stuff just happen in America and not in Scotland—a question I entertained for a few short minutes? After all, it would have been easier to blame this on America than on my lack of insight and awareness. Growing up in Scotland in a predominantly Caucasian and Christian community, I somehow managed to remain oblivious to the myriad of diversity issues that was actually surrounding me.

The more I ruminated about the insights I gained during that week-long seminar in Bethel, Maine, the more I realized the 32 years of my life prior must have been filled with stories I was missing, so I set out to unpack a few memories and look closely in the rear view mirror.

When I was 12 years old, I found myself in "Inclusion Limbo;" I did not know it then and certainly would not have described it as such, but that is exactly what it was. My maternal grandmother lived in the Miners Rows, a working class part of town where all the coal miners lived. My aunt on my father's side lived in a more upscale part of town in a bungalow, or single-family home. When I visited my maternal grandmother, I would stand at her window and watch the children playing on the street and think to myself, I did not ever want to be part of that group. My father used to relentlessly tease my mother about coming from "The Miners Rows," and I am guessing that message of being lower working class stuck to me like Velcro.

On most Sunday afternoons, we visited my aunt's house on my father's side. I distinctly recall one Sunday standing alone in the back garden when a neighbor raised her kitchen window and invited me to come inside and play with her daughter. I shook my head no and never moved. Part of me wanted to go, but I did not feel good enough to play with upper class kids because I felt I did not belong there either. We lived in a tenement building and they lived in a bungalow. The social distance from the Miners Rows to the tenement to the bungalow was such a wide chasm in my teenage mind that the barriers could not be crossed, or at least my feet would not take me in either direction. This was exclusion by choice on both occasions, but apparently for very different and juxtaposed reasons.

It turns out inclusion and I have been in a delicate dance together for many years. A trusted advisor once told me if something happens once, it is an accident; twice, it is a coincidence; and the third time, it is a pattern. As I peer through an inclusion lens at my own history and patterns, I see my relationships with significant others and my need to be accepted by them has blinded me for too long. There were plenty of overt and covert messages and signals that suggested moving on sooner than I did. Sometimes, we try too hard to be included, often to our own detriment. Hence, another dimension of human nature to wrestle with.

Self-help books abound with topics either directly or closely related to our need to be accepted. Toxic relationships survive longer than they should, because people do not cut the ties and walk away. This is true whether you stay too long in a relationship or stay too long in the wrong job. My own journey to understand the rejected part of myself continues to inform my work. I listen to my inner voice. I catch the relentless ticker-tape of conversations in my head; the good, the bad, and the ugly, and I realize if these things live in my body, they live in yours. This awareness and mindfulness consciously and unconsciously feeds my passion to help others achieve a more inclusive world. It is said, we teach what we want to learn, and increasingly I realize how true that is.

The Pathology of Inclusion

Back in Bethel, Maine, one of the Black male facilitators shared his view that things would not change for Black Americans or People of Color until White people stood up and became accountable for their part of the story. Back then, I was not entirely sure what that entailed. My somewhat naïve response to that "call to action" was to believe I could develop and sell a workshop on "White Awareness." Of course, I was never able to sell that particular topic, but it was the beginning of my professional interest and passion for diversity and inclusion.

My initial burst of enthusiasm was quickly dashed by the resistance we met in workshops when talking about diversity. Participants did not always want to be there. We had volunteers and victims in every workshop; people who wanted to be there and people who felt forced to be. I began to realize while it may seem intuitively obvious, we should all behave inclusively that is not how the story generally unfolds. Resistance manifest in many forms, from eye rolling to folded arms, "shut-down" body language and overt challenges to the workshop process. In one workshop, which I can picture to this day, a very large White man pushed his employee ID badge close to my face and said he would stay in the room, but refused to participate. He then walked to the back of the room, pulled up a chair, put his feet on a table; and began to read a book. His visible rejection of the workshop caused more than a small ripple effect, particularly when four of his White male colleagues joined him and we continued to "ignore" them. The next day, to make a strong learning point, all the African American participants joined them at the back of the room, bringing the workshop to a temporary halt as we untangled the disarray. You can imagine the impact this had on inclusion. The lessons learned were never lost on me as I realized that my personal feelings of being intimidated on day 1 had blinded me to the racial inequities we had inadvertently created in the workshop. On another occasion, I recall a man sitting in the workshop with his briefcase on his lap. He refused to participate in any of the activities and kept his hands flat on his briefcase and stared straight ahead. At one point, he rose and left the room and reappeared two hours later. I managed to hold it together throughout the workshop. But that evening at dinner as I recounted his behavior, I was reduced to tears as I realized the tension he created by ostensibly doing nothing and yet, making his resistance and presence felt. When there is an elephant in the room, it is hard to feel the comfort of inclusion.

You might think at this juncture that the blame for lack of inclusion sits squarely on the shoulders of people in the dominant culture(s), namely White, male, heterosexual, and Christian. Nothing could be further from the truth. We all own a piece of the story. The underlying pathologies and characteristics of human nature are stuck to us like Velcro and render us unable to be at peace and fully inclusive.

In our workshops, these stories showed up again and again—sometimes, it was a woman who expressed her resistance to being labeled a "woman." Sometimes, it was a person of color or member of the LGBTI (lesbian, gay, bi-sexual, trans-gender and inter-sex) community, who preferred to disassociate from their group and resented being asked to talk about it. I recall one gay male being very angry at his gay colleagues who chose to stay in the closet. He was harder on them than on any other group. Repeatedly people would tell us they did not want to be labeled as a member of *any* group. They preferred to be seen as "just an individual." But that is not as simple as it sounds.

Just as there are two sides to every coin, the issue is not only how you want to be seen, but how others see you and what they project on you.

You may be a gay male and want to be known simply as "Michael, the individual," but if other people know you are gay, they have their own story and incumbent behavior they align with that story—none of which you have any control over.

An Unhealthy Longing for Inclusion

It goes without saying the need to be included or the propensity to exclude others does not limit itself to discussions in carefully bounded and structured Diversity workshops. We want to believe we always behave professionally. But, the behavioral choices we make are more likely to be situation or relationship-dependent and influenced by a myriad of factors. These factors include our affinity for some people over others. Inclusion dynamics are messy and complex and the ramifications overflow into our business relationships. They lurk under the surface and show up in how we feel about ourselves, how we treat others, and how we allow ourselves to be treated.

My underlying need to feel included caused me to spend many years being too accommodating in all facets of my life. Where did that come from? What was the driving force? Perhaps it all began with children's nursery rhymes and axioms from the past—"Sugar and Spice and all things nice, that is what little girls are made of" or the often-heard "Little girls should be seen and not heard," but wherever I received the mental memes and mind viruses it infiltrated my DNA in such a way it became the backdrop to important decisions. I continued for countless years to not find my own voice in significant relationships, until I was willing to step back and look at it as a chronic and systemic pattern.

Being a people pleaser, being too accommodating, cognitively rationalizing or justifying egregious behavior, and a willingness to assimilate to the needs of others at our own expense are all signals of an unhealthy longing for inclusion. It is part of our human nature to have these fallibilities and to have them show up as a barrier to being inclusive in a healthy way.

Indeed, it is also human nature for other people not to want to include us because they see our imperfections and don't want to deal with them. All of these human characteristics, flaws, and idiosyncrasies can throw a wrench into the very idea that we are striving for a more inclusive work-place, but they are an inextricable part of the story.

The bottom line is we all have a story to tell about how and why we are not willing to be inclusive of others. Understanding that, forgiving ourselves and forgiving others is part of our challenge. But, overcoming that isn't always about getting rid of your reluctance to be inclusive; it is about having more acceptance and bandwidth for others. You may not have the privilege of knowing someone else's story, but you should at least entertain that they have an underlying story. What is your story?

A Healthy Desire for Inclusion

Given it is part of our inherent human nature to struggle with inclusion, what could a healthy desire for inclusion look like? Is it even possible? It is, but to do so, we have to put the skunk on the table. We have to be honest with ourselves and admit we are not always thinking inclusively.

In a world of inclusion are we sometimes allowed to not be inclusive? Maybe we don't always want to be inclusive of difference. Maybe it is OK to hang out with our "own group" on occasions, but doing so in the full knowledge when we are in diverse groups, we have to figure out how to be more inclusive. And that takes more work than you think.

When I find myself with a group of my Scottish or British friends, I breathe differently. There is a comfort level and a repartee unique to our customs and culture. When we are all together, it is easy for that to surface freely. Everyone intuitively understands the sarcasm, the humor, and the in-jokes. When I am with other groups I tend to hold back on expressing my views and opinions. I rein in my sense of humor for fear the sarcasm or innuendo will be misunderstood.

Of course, I could easily make the case we are *always* in diverse groups due to personality differences, quirks and foibles we all display even in seemingly homogenous groups. Alternatively, I could claim we are all just individuals. Some of the pushback we hear during Diversity workshops is that people do not want to be labeled members of a group; they want to be seen as an individual. The problem is both things are simultaneously true. You are an individual and a member of diverse groups, and you are also seen by others as both as well. We may think we are looking at a tower of giraffes, but every giraffe has a unique pattern, which brings me full circle back to the illusion of inclusion and our need to more fully understand the complexity.

We are not inclusive every moment of our lives and we don't need to be. Raising this to consciousness puts inclusion under a magnifying glass, seeking the best solutions, when we do need to be inclusive. We must unravel our fears and anxieties about difference and become curious and engaged authentically and courageously. We must be willing to at least question some of our long and tightly held beliefs about ourselves and others.

Learning how to be diversity-sensitive and inclusive is an ongoing challenge. I realized many years ago that there is no end point. There are no shortcuts, and no time when you can tell yourself your job is done. It is a journey, and vigilance and self-reflection need to be your constant companion. As with Maslow's Hierarchy—you never quite self-actualize and you can slip back down the ladder. It is part of the process to make mistakes and take some chances in order to reach across the divide of difference and learn about each other. It is important to admit none of us is a perfect human being and to know there are moments or days we just do not have our diversity hat on straight.

Perhaps most of all, we have to forgive ourselves, accept our human frailty, and be willing to work on ourselves; to be mindful and inwardly reflective before we look outside. Socrates said, "The unexamined life is not worth living," and our ability to resolve the inclusion paradox will depend on our ability to live the "examined life" and to realize our unchallenged brain is not always worth trusting.

We Are Individuals AND a member of groups
What group do you feel most comfortable with?
It is a journey, there is no end-point

CHAPTER 1

The Bottom Line: The Real Deal on Inclusion

We say we want inclusion but what if we really don't?

We work at being inclusive, but we never quite arrive. Perhaps we have unconscious beliefs at odds with what we say we want—a hidden agenda that deters and detracts from our consciously stated desires.

Inclusion is complex. It is in our human nature not to be liberally inclusive or, at the very least, to be skeptical of it. The challenges of inclusion arise from human problems that come from human situations and have to be explored in a human way. Inclusion is not merely a program to be implemented; it is an inherently human characteristic with many complex variables, twists, and turns. That is why it is probable we are *not really trying* to be inclusive; we only think we are.

Selfishness and Altruism—The Odd Couple

What does inclusivity look like? What do I mean by selfishness as it relates to inclusion? What does altruism have to do with inclusion?

My vision of inclusivity does not include all of us being inclusive all of the time. It is a more measured and realistic look at what is possible. It is an ability to be more open to inclusivity while at the same time more fully understanding the parameters and boundaries that limit us. Pragmatically speaking, perhaps we don't really understand what inclusivity is and the sacrifices it entails. We don't have a firm grasp on what it could look like and maybe are not hard-wired to be inclusive. Despite the humor, the old adage, "Ok enough about me, why don't you talk about me now?" holds more than a grain of truth. We are inherently selfish. Yet we can be led toward altruism. Altruism is defined as the disinterested and selfless concern for the well-being of others. When I think about altruism,

Mother Teresa comes to mind, but most of us don't even get close to that standard.

But altruism is actually not part of the equation when we strive to be more inclusive at work. Inclusion programs at work are driven by the desire to improve team work, productivity, creativity, innovation and profit and subsequently reap an improved Return on Investment (ROI) for the company. And while we individually have the potential to be altruistic, we are actually predisposed to be selfish; to think about ourselves first, to relate everything back to ourselves and seek to protect ourselves and our territory. A few years ago one of my clients moved from a hierarchical management system to empowered work teams. As part of that change, they opened an activity-based building where employees were expected to work on a hot-desking system, without their own defined workspace. However, people quickly claimed their favorite space and brought personal artifacts from home to mark their territory. Many meetings over many months were needed to educate people *not* to mark their own lamp post.

Why does it take us so long to change, even when we say we want to? Our brain habituates. It is much more comfortable finding patterns, making sense of them, and sticking to them. Our unconscious brain processes 200,000 times more information than the conscious mind and is constantly looking for patterns. When it finds them, it wires them together; this is a process of which we are not consciously aware (Jones and Cornish 2015). These patterns, red flags, and conflicting feelings permeate our unconscious. In addition, our invisible "rules for inclusion" show up in many ways both at home and work. We can be well-meaning and work diligently toward creating a more inclusive workplace *and yet* fail to achieve our stated goals. In large part, this is because our internal programming is designed to be selective and cautious about whom we let in to our inner circle and on what terms they can join.

Speaking of patterns, I have found most people do not feel comfortable with the idea they may be to blame for any form of discrimination toward others; often separating in their minds how they show up at work with their professional faces from how they show up in the privacy of their own homes and communities. At a recent dinner party I overheard one of the dinner guests saying "The Blacks in this country should be grateful; they don't know how good they've got it." My eyebrows shot up as I leaned forward to listen intently, eventually intervening with my own perspective. The people talking believed they were decent people and good neighbors, who were not prejudiced. In their defense, one of them was quick to say that they have Black neighbors and another that her new grand-daughter has a Black father, as if those explanations gave them permission to fragment their thinking and exempted them from bias.

The views expressed at the dinner party are not isolated, unique, or limited to one group. It is part of the human condition and the issues of inclusion and exclusion run deep. And I am sure you can somehow relate to this story. We all have many sides to our personalities and many different faces we show to the world.

Dr. Peter Jones, a Professor at Cambridge University Neuro Science Department (Jones and Cornish 2015) said, even if you consciously reject a stereotype, it will lie dormant in neural pathways waiting to be activated; just like data sits on your hard drive waiting to be accessed. For instance, it's a safe bet when you were a child, your parents told you to forget about something biased you heard. Try as you might, the message was already received and dropped into the neural pathways, lying dormant waiting for opportunities to remind you of it. We take in mind viruses and form mental models of people and situations without realizing it. In fact, Dr. Jones says that frequently using a particular cognitive pathway increases the likelihood it will get used again. This is done by coating the nerve ending with a substance called myelin, which increases the efficiency of activation of that route by up to 5,000 times. Just seeing or hearing a stereotype increases the myelination even if you consciously reject it. Your brain is lazy and always likes to have the complete picture. If the information is missing, it will seek to fill it with the most likely fit. Your biases are often used to fill in the gaps. My friends at the dinner party were able to convince themselves of their inherent goodness and tolerance, while unconsciously tapping into those knotty, or do I mean naughty, myelinated messages. Assumptions of affinity and shared values were underpinning the conversation at the dinner party in question. While they cannot be removed, you can learn to catch them and be mindful of the choices you make going forward.

Sometimes we assume as we look around the room that we have affinity with others, without knowing their unique story. Often, the speaker does not give any thought to the pain caused by throwaway comments and do not realize their words might be hurting others. We see a group that "looks like us," and we unconsciously assume shared values. We may not know that someone's son is gay or married to someone from another culture. We see someone who looks White, but they are really Latino or Black. Comments are made about members of different groups or people's characteristics (height, weight, and so on) with the implicit assumption that everyone in the assembled gathering agrees. Frequently that is not the case and as the old adage says, "Once the words are out of your mouth, they are out of your control."

A UCLA study by Naomi Eisenberger and Matthew Lieberman discovered that the part of the brain that experiences pain when you cut your finger is the same part activated and agitated when you feel excluded. They hooked a student up to a Functional Magnetic Resonance Imaging machine (fMRI) and had him take part in a computer simulation game throwing the ball to two other people. After about 10 minutes of inclusion in this exercise he was then excluded, and was never thrown the ball again. The act of being excluded showed up in his brain patterns as a physiological reaction (Eisenberger, Lieberman, and Williams 2003). The study further concluded that taking a painkiller minimized the pain of exclusion just as it reduces the pain when you cut your finger. I am not recommending you do that however, it explains how being excluded is painful to the individual and a productivity drain on the organization. *Exclusion = physical pain*

Self-Sabotage—An Unconscious Plan for Failure and the Protection of the Status Quo

When we talk about being inclusive of difference, do we really act like this is something we want—or is it just something we think we should do? Do we unconsciously sabotage it because, in our hearts, the effort is too much? Are we dubious as to whether it is even possible? We are driven by the desire to be in relationship with others, but we consciously and unconsciously work to surround ourselves with people who share our values, beliefs, and behaviors that make us comfortable. In other words, we are only really comfortable including people who are either like us or are willing to do what it takes to fit in with us.

You may work in a diverse team, and you may be able to look around the organization and visibly see diverse people, but can you swear you know and understand all of their individual differences and underlying stories? Do you really, deep down, want to know more about diversity?

Over the years, many well-meaning leaders have told me they do not care about a person's diversity, so long as they can do the job. They do not take the time to know their story. They do not care if they are purple with polka dots, so long as they can do the job. On these occasions, I ask, "But what if *they* care?" What if it matters to *them* and they would feel more able to be productive at work if they felt you understood their background?

There are a myriad of ways to send a message to your team you are not interested in who they are or what they have to say. These micro-messages are heard loud and clear not just by the individual concerned, but the entire team witnessing the exchange.

We unconsciously protect our territory and the status quo by shutting out other voices and styles. If we let them in, we might have to listen to them. We might have to adopt different ways of doing things; listen to different music, dance to a different tune, and eat different food. Are you really OK encouraging diverse voices, listening to diverse views and opinions, and implementing other ideas instead of your own?

I worked a few years ago with a client who was implementing an internal diversity awareness workshop based on the Diversity Onion or Diversity Wheel. The inner core of the onion contains social identity groups such as race, culture, gender, sexual orientation, age, and so on; the second circle contains issues such as family status, religious beliefs, marital status, military service, personality types, and so on; and the outer rim contains business issues such as functional groups, length of service, geographical location, and so on.

During a discussion with the training team about the impact of the workshop, a woman of color shared that she and her colleagues attended

ELEPHANT

the workshop hoping they would finally have their voices heard. However, they found the facilitators were teaching the workshop from the outer rim of the Diversity Dimension model with only an occasional sojourn into the second circle and never ever putting their toes into the deeper waters at the core of the model where race, culture, gender, sexual orientation, and age lived.

She expressed disappointment that she and her colleagues were not able to share what it means to be a person of color at work. The message this sent to the participants was deafening.

The facilitators' personal need to stay within their own comfort level and the unconscious collusion of many of the participants ensured the conversation stayed at a safe and superficial level. The outcome was that diverse views were not heard and differing opinions were not encouraged. Comfort and the status quo were maintained, ironically while still posturing as a Diversity and Inclusion initiative.

On another occasion, I observed a gay White male facilitator completely bypass a comment from an African American woman, ostensibly in the interests of moving on with the agenda. She raised her hand and shared that she felt isolated in the organization and was often the only Black person in a meeting. The facilitator thanked her and said, "That is interesting" and moved to the next topic. Her eyes got wide and she dropped her head in a slump of resignation and disappointment. There it is again, our inability to stay in the moment, hold someone's gaze, and try to understand the depth of what they are saying. These are not isolated incidents. We are all capable of doing this and stories abound as to the many ways we can "move on" and select not to see or hear an opinion different from our own, particularly if it makes us feel anxious or fearful. If you do not believe me, think about your significant relationships at home. How often do you anticipate what your partner or spouse is about to say? How often do you cut them off at the pass or mentally roll your eyes and stop listening?

We want to do well, but we are often blinded by the light of our own intrinsic biases, while, at the same time, believing it is not us causing the lack of progress. The problem remains; if we are all being "well-intentioned" and telling ourselves it is not us, who is it?

Protecting Our Turf and Checking the Box

Why are we not achieving our stated goal? Why have we not closed the gender gap? Why are women and people of color not moving up the corporate ladder in significant numbers? Why do we have such a long journey ahead of us to get some diverse groups onto the leadership radar screen? Organizations pour money and resources into Diversity and Inclusion initiatives, and yet many companies are still spinning their wheels around the inclusion axis.

The crux of the problem is we don't begin to appreciate the layers of convolution. We don't always realize when we are not being inclusive. While it is part of human nature to want to be in relationship with others, inclusivity does not come naturally. It is not intuitive to accommodate differences. For example, we marry people for their difference and then spend the rest of the relationship trying to change them to be more like us. Companies do the same as they hire for diversity and manage for similarity. We fill our departments with diverse people, but never fully utilize their uniqueness. In fact, we directly and indirectly influence and acculturate them to minimize their differences in order to fit in. People of difference are complicit in this process as they want to belong, so we are all accomplices to the process that keeps us stuck. We may believe that we are being inclusive and genuinely not see or understand how much accommodation other people are making to ensure we are comfortable. Women, for example, are told to be more assertive, and are often sent to assertiveness training but, when they comply and try out their new found assertiveness, they run the risk of being labeled too aggressive or with other less flattering labels.

In many ways, we are checking the box to say we have done something while simultaneously maintaining the status quo; protecting our turf and maintaining our comfort levels.

How many managers do you know who are excellent listeners, who consciously work to ensure everyone's voice is heard, who point out to the group when someone is interrupted or when someone takes another person's ideas and claims them as their own? You might be tempted to proclaim, "But this happens to everyone and has nothing to do with diversity and inclusion"; but it does. Part of being inclusive is about how you treat people. The business meeting agenda may be the object of our attention, but people roll their eyes in meetings and gossip outside of meetings because of how they get treated and how they see others treated.

While it is spot-on that these things can happen to anyone, stories abound from women and people of color within organizations who know their voices are not heard as credible. The problem is more systemic and chronic than just a few people not being heard. Global research results from my unconscious bias assessment tool, Cognizant, show a consistently wide gap between dominant culture groups and subcultural groups on the issue of whose voice is heard as credible and whose ideas are more likely to be implemented. The example on this chart is only looking at the functional differences between revenue generating employees and support staff, but similar gaps exist in gender, race, culture, sexual orientation, and so on. Why does that happen if we say we want to be inclusive? Why does it happen if your team is already diverse? It happens because we lean toward affinity bias, and the status quo, and also because we are not always aware of what we are doing.

I had lunch with someone recently and every time I agreed with what she was saying, she emphatically proclaimed "No, no no; *really*, I am serious." I was quite startled when she first did it as I was actually agreeing with her. But, as she continued to manifest that behavior I became used to it; anticipated it and later speculated that her job as a school teacher may have unconsciously influenced her to need to keep reinforcing her point with the students. Of course, I really don't know why she does it and maybe one day I will ask her.

These anecdotal examples of understanding differences and being inclusive illustrate that it is more challenging and complicated than it first appears. Do we really know when we get it right or when we offend? Are we aware when we are holding back and avoiding conversations about differences? Do we really want to know the other person's story, particularly if it might clash with the story we have in our head? Do we render diverse individuals who become our friends as phenomenological exceptions and yet still have challenges with their diverse group? Does all of this complexity make us opt for political correctness? Do we save our bias

Functional Groups and Inclusion

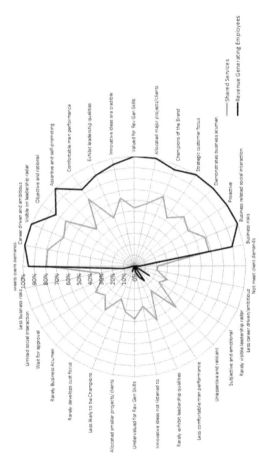

© Human Facets (2014)

conversations until we are with close friends and/or people we assume will have affinity with us?

Over the years of working on Diversity and Inclusion, I have witnessed countless situations and heard numerous stories confirming that what we say in public and in private, or indeed are really thinking, may lack congruency. Perhaps you have experienced being with people from your own affinity group who take it for granted everyone in the assembled gathering agrees with their stated views and biases about other diverse groups. I am Scottish and for a few years, in the early 1970s, I lived in Wales. It was not uncommon at that time for Welsh people to make disparaging jokes about the English and they would often make the assumption that, because of my Celtic roots, I shared their views. I did not, and while it was often done with an element of good-hearted sarcasm and repartee, "We Celts must stick together," it grew old to have people assume that I agreed with them. This phenomenon is not new and not limited to cultural diversity.

Things Change and Remain the Same

We have been working diligently on Diversity and Inclusion since the 1980s, and things have certainly improved and yet, in many ways remain the same. We have not really made much progress on the substantive issues. We are certainly more accepting of the idea we are diverse and we should value diversity and have diverse teams. We seem to understand the importance of recruiting diverse people and ensuring our recruiters are diverse, but are we any closer to having equal pay for women? Are we any closer to shattering the glass ceiling for women or people or color? Are there more women on boards? Do we have more openly LGBTI people in leadership? Do you see more differently abled people in your workplace? Are we more able to have courageous conversations about differences with people from different diverse groups and provide constructive feedback to all people, regardless of their diversity? With all the money that has been invested in Diversity and Inclusion programs and all the passionate efforts from Diversity and Inclusion professionals, including leaders who stepped up to be champions, how can we not have made more progress? Not to mention the employees who participate in Employee Resource groups and attend Diversity week conferences, lunch and learn events, and workshops. It begs the question whether we have just been paying lip service to the issue? The words of Jean-Baptiste Alphonse Karr (*Les Guêpes*, January 1849) come to mind—"plus ça change, plus c'est la même chose" usually translated as "the more things change, the more they stay the same" (Karr 1849). The late Wayne Dyer is also quoted as saying, "If you change the way you look at things, the things you look at change" (Dyer 2004), and I suggest that is what we must do if we really want to move the needle on inclusion. We must look at the complexity of inclusion through a different lens and begin to unpack and address the many dimensions that block us from being inclusive, personally, professionally, and at an organizational and societal level. This is a journey not for the faint of heart, but I have confidence that once we can clearly see the path ahead and have the correct GPS or roadmap in our hands, we will be willing to take large and definitive strides toward the road less traveled; intent this time on *expanding* the box and not just *checking* the box.

References

Dyer, W. 2004. *The Power of Intention*. USA: Hay House Inc.

Eisenberger, N.I., M.D. Lieberman, and K.D. Williams. October 2003. "Does Rejection Hurt: An fMRI Study of Social Exclusion." *Science* 302, pp. 290–92.

Jones, C., and T. Cornish. 2015. Unconscious Bias Fact Sheet.

Karr, J.-B.A. 1849. *Les Guepes*. Paris, France.

CHAPTER 2

Inclusion Ground Hog Day: Stop Spinning Your Wheels

Why have we not yet solved the gender pay gap? Why are there not more women and People of Color on corporate boards? Why is there not more diversity within the ranks of the C-suite? Why have we not leveled the playing field or tapped into the creativity and innovation that diversity portends to offer?

There are different ways of looking at these questions. Either we know we have not made real progress, but are not sure what to do about it or we don't realize we have a problem because we believe we are doing quite well with diversity and inclusion. After all, we are always talking about it. Or, we tell ourselves things are much better than they used to be. Or, we watch the news and realize we might actually be regressing nationally and globally.

I think a little bit of all of that is true. Yes, we have made progress and yet, paradoxically, things are regressing. I occasionally catch myself sighing with silent resignation, shrugging my shoulders and wondering "what's the point; this will never get fixed." Thankfully, these moments are few and often times help to level set me for the road ahead. For the people who are tired of talking about diversity and those who believe one day we will arrive at a place where we can stop talking about it, I have a news flash. We will never reach that day. This journey never ends, and there will always be work to be done. As one of my esteemed consulting colleagues used to say, "there is no there there." We might change some of the issues or put the focus on different groups over time, but we will never reach an inclusion panacea or diversity nirvana. That is not a reason to stop trying, however.

When I think about the illusion of inclusion, the journey from unconscious incompetence to unconscious competence comes to mind.

We don't know what we don't know, and solving the inclusion puzzle is like walking into a maze using a Rubik Cube as your roadmap and then wondering why you are lost.

A Convoluted Maze

As convoluted and challenging as this maze is, we need to look at inclusivity at a much deeper level, if we intend to master it. It is not just a "check the box" exercise. We need to roll up our sleeves and grapple with the details as that is where we will find the secrets to solving the inclusion Rubik Cube.

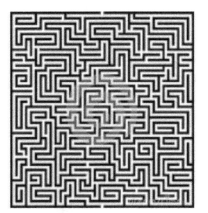

Where does the maze begin? In some ways, the answer is "how long is a piece of string." However, let's take our first steps along the road less traveled.

Women have long been the gateway to the launch of Corporate Diversity and Inclusion programs. Fixing the gender gap has been seen as the beginning of the maze since we began tackling diversity and inclusion eons ago. The acknowledged and indisputable challenge surrounding equal pay, promotion, and retention of women created a perfect storm. Executives and senior leaders were convinced of the business case by compelling demographic data carefully prepared and presented by the human resource departments. Corporate dashboards show the lack of women in the board room, pay inequity, and an inability to retain and promote women in representative numbers. These facts adequately established a burning platform, and a business imperative was born, justifying the launch of a gender initiative.

Gender may have seemed like the obvious starting place because the data showed it clearly needed to be addressed. But another less obvious and more unconscious part of the story is it was easier and less threatening than tackling some other more sensitive issues, such as race or sexual orientation. I have had numerous conversations with HR professionals and Diversity departments who said:

> "We *only* want to focus on gender."
> "Our leaders are not ready to address other issues."
> "Our leaders would not be comfortable discussing sexual orientation."
> "We are planning to hold race, culture, sexual orientation and other issues on the back-burner until we reach our gender goals."

When I think about rolling out Inclusion programs, my mind goes to architecture and the difference between load-bearing pillars and decorative pillars, which are used merely as a façade. Successful initiatives need to be built on load-bearing pillars. It is mission-critical that the C-suite, executive leaders, and managers become authentic champions and active supporters. Lip service is not an option and will be seen for what it is—a façade or window dressing. Money and resources will be wasted while maintaining the status quo.

The hope of the HR community is once their leaders see the business imperative; they will take the reins and begin to shape the direction of travel. These leaders will encourage other leaders and managers to climb aboard, successfully cascading the D and I change initiatives throughout the organization. In the process, a considerable amount of energy is expended by the HR professionals and Diversity and Inclusion leaders to ensure they do not unnerve their leadership. They also must worry about how to successfully engage the "frozen middle"—the managers and supervisors at the front line, who can support or derail any initiatives. Questions that are front of mind for most Chief Diversity Officers and HR leadership include:

1. What compelling evidence can we provide to prove there is a business case?
2. How can we ensure our leaders get "it?"
3. How can we recruit our leaders to be active champions and ambassadors for this change initiative?

4. How can we persuade our leaders to own this program and not see it as an HR issue?

5. How can we appeal to both their heads and their hearts?

6. What guidance can we provide to ensure our leaders are proactive in promoting events and are seen to "walk the talk?"

7. How can we provide measurements to ensure we make a compelling and water-tight case for action?

8. How can we avoid the pitfalls and obstacles that might cause our leaders to put the brakes on?

9. How do we manage resistance to this initiative? How do we engage the "frozen middle?"

10. What would scare our leaders into backing off?

11. What would encourage our leaders to maintain forward momentum?

12. What do we need to do to win corporate awards for our efforts?

Just looking at the questions that lie under the surface of a yet to be launched Diversity initiative begins to disclose the complexity and the anxiety. It does not take long to realize this effort cannot be contained as a neat and tidy linear journey. Waiting to complete one segment properly (e.g., gender) before progressing to the next will not work and does not facilitate arriving at the desired end point of inclusion. All diverse groups, including heterosexual, Christian White men, and members of other dominant groups, must be included in the conversation. The challenge is to understand what "being included in the conversation" really involves. How do we ensure all voices are heard and everyone becomes comfortable with differences? Do people believe their unique diversity story is being heard and their group is being included in the conversation?

'Holistic, not piecemeal'

Sharing the Pie

One reason we have not made more progress is we are all consciously and unconsciously holding on to our psychological territory and our inalienable right to have things remain the same. We may accept things are changing around us, but we don't really feel comfortable with the world within our sphere of influence changing. The winds of change are not easy and certainly test our limitations and boundaries in unexpected ways. When I moved countries, I did not for a minute factor if it was going to change who I was and how I thought about the world, after all, I am Scottish, born and bred.

In stark contrast to the weather I grew up with, the warm air of Miami washed over me as I stepped off the British Airways flight that brought me from my native country of Scotland to my new home in the United States.

George Bernard Shaw is reported to have said, "England and America are two nations divided by a common language." Arriving in the United States of America in 1980, I quickly became aware that everything I previously took for granted in the United Kingdom could no longer be assumed to be true. In the early months, I felt like an outsider, wondering how long it would be before I stopped thinking I was driving on the "wrong" side of the road. I experienced what George Bernard Shaw implied and to this day, some 36 years later, I still bump up against cultural norms and expectations different from the mental models I carried since childhood. Our cultural messages and conditioning remain with us and never go away. To this day, I am not comfortable in eating dinner early. "Early Bird" specials are an enigma to me still; a little voice inside me says "This is just too strange—who eats dinner at 5.30 p.m.; High Tea perhaps, but not dinner." The fact that our cultural messages are so deeply rooted and often operating at an unconscious level is part of the complexity of inclusion. After years of living in the United States, I find myself often culturally challenged. Most of the time, I feel I am unconsciously and consciously being an American, and other times, I am reminded I am really Scottish. When it comes to sports, I am always rooting for U.S. teams in my favorite global sports of golf and tennis. When the Ryder Cup Golf Tournament is happening, I passionately cheer for the U.S. team; ecstatic when they win and dejected when they lose. My European golfing friends are often offended as I am not supporting my European countrymen.

Cultural roots run deep and remind me in some ways of barnacles. Barnacles have one defining life decision. That is where they are going to live. Once they make that decision, they spend the rest of their lives with their head cemented to the same rock. My experience as an immigrant has shown me that while you may live your life with one foot firmly planted in your country of residence and one firmly planted in your country of origin, your head remains cemented to the original rock. Over time, you adapt to your new country's values and norms, but your country of origin continues its magnetic pull over you. The strong connections and values of your birthplace never leave your body.

For instance, in Scotland, we do not start celebrating New Year until the stroke of midnight on New Year's Eve. It is said we keep celebrating (aka drinking) until Rabbie Burns Day on January 25. It is considered inappropriate, even bad luck, to wish people a Happy New Year before the Bells (midnight on New Year's Eve). Even after 36 years, I never managed to become comfortable with the fact that people in the United States wish me "Happy New Year" days before it happens. I cringe every time they do it as if I am ducking to avoid the bolt of lightning that inevitably comes with disrespecting that time-honored tradition. On those occasions, I relate to the barnacle as my head remains stuck to the same rock that lies somewhere on the seashore in Kirn, Scotland, where I spent my formative years. This may seem trivial, but the feelings are incredibly real. And, feelings are essentially what drive most of our behavior, for right or wrong, when it comes to inclusion.

Grappling with the Rubik Cube

One of my sisters and my niece and nephew are brilliant at solving the Rubik cube puzzle; they seem to intuitively know what to do to make it twist and turn its way into conformity and order. I, on the other hand, look at it with a defeated glare, knowing no matter how hard I try, I will never figure out how to get all the colors neatly aligned and separated by "sides." The very thought of even picking it up makes my stomach turn. Grappling with the "inclusion Rubik Cube," on the other hand, is right up my alley.

I own three Rubik Cubes—one of them has all of the colors separated by sides, the second has a mix of colors on each side, and the third one has a different beautiful pattern on each side—I did not make any of that happen—I must have bought them that way and they remain blissfully untouched. However, they are the perfect reminder of the three worlds I see before me—a world where we all live separately, a world where we can be perfectly integrated, and a world where we can tap into the creativity and innovation of our differences to produce an even more beautiful reality. Paradoxically, in deciding to wrestle the

inclusion Rubik Cube to the ground, we would not be aiming at separating colors into "sides," nor would we want to melt it down into one big happy rainbow sherbet hodge-podge. Ideally, we want a healthy mix of colors and shapes that work in harmony together. As I am sure you have guessed, getting there will be more complicated than moving the pieces on a Rubik Cube.

Magic Potions, Fairy Dust, and Reality

Steve Jobs said, "Simple can be harder than complex." When it comes to achieving the goal of an inclusive work environment, there are many interconnected variables and yet, simple solutions may be hidden in plain sight. There are no magic potions or sprinklings of fairy dust to help us become more inclusive. The key to having a more inclusive workplace will be found in understanding what I refer to as the *immutable and permeable forces*. These forces are omnipresent and always at play. They conspire to keep us spinning our wheels. Separately they are daunting and together they are an impassable force. In order to win the day on inclusion, we must raise awareness of these forces and attempt to see more clearly what may already be in front of our eyes. Similar to being introduced to the mischievous and adventuresome Three Musketeers, let me now introduce you to the impenetrable characteristics of the three immutable forces.

CHAPTER 3

Hard-Mired: The Immutable Forces of Inclusion

Immutable Forces

© Human Facets 2016

Just as there are immutable laws of nature, there are immutable forces at play with inclusion. An immutable force is fixed and cannot be changed. There are things about inclusivity that are totally inorganic and our resistance to these things can be so deeply engrained that it would seem we are mired in it and forever destined to act against inclusion. This is particularly true when the gap between the perceived differences is too wide or the numbers become too large.

I recall being in a conversation with some British friends a few years ago. We were discussing cricket, where England was playing against India, and the conversation turned to the increased number of Indians and Pakistanis living in different British cities. My friends lived in a quiet, predominantly English suburb, a few hours south of London. They told me they would not object to an Indian or Pakistani family living in their street. When I asked them to imagine every family on the street other than them was from another culture, their attitude changed and they became visibly uncomfortable.

Working to be more inclusive is hard and goes against our nature. Your head tells you that you should think more inclusively, but your heart takes you on a knee-jerking emotional journey every time the inclusion boundary is tested. You tell yourself you want a more inclusive workplace, and yet, when you shop for groceries and see the food labels in another language, your mind goes into overload. Before you know it, Darth Vader takes over your brain cells and you feel threatened by the thought "they" are taking over. A simple act, a complex reaction, and an even deeper immutable challenge to your, albeit unconscious, sense of privilege, and dominance.

Going Against Our Nature

"Will the last American leaving please bring the flag."

The first time I heard someone say that I was startled and confused. I did not know what they meant. It turns out they were referring to "White Flight" in South Florida, where in recent years, there has been a large increase in the Latino/Hispanic population and an increasing number of White people moving north. When I was teaching as an adjunct professor at the business school of a local university, I heard students say they wanted to go back home as it was "too diverse" down here. Diversity workshops we ran in the 90s would go really well so long as we had only a few people of color present. White participants appreciated hearing the stories from people of color and felt they gained insights and perspectives they had not previously known. But, when a workshop had close to 50 percent, the dynamics changed. White participants went from being interested in the stories to feeling anxious. They told us later they had been comfortable with the Black people they worked with until they attended the workshop and were forced to talk about diversity. When I facilitated Diversity workshops for a major corporate client in a small town in Minnesota, the participants complained too many Asian people had moved into their neighborhood making them feel less safe.

Does it really go against our human nature to be inclusive of others? Will we ever overcome our need to close ranks against *too much* difference? Does a celebration of difference need to be on our terms? And, who is in charge of writing the terms and conditions?

Evidence abounds it is in our human nature to want to be kind, considerate, and inclusive of others. Events like the Olympics opening and closing ceremonies bring us together in celebration of our differences, and television ads sell products on the back of the message "We are the world," convincing us diversity brings beauty and joy. In these moments, we wrap our hands around a warm cup of our favorite beverage, curl up in front of the fire, and enjoy experiencing a cozy feeling and a sense of hope.

Yet evidence also surrounds us every day that it runs contrary to our human nature to include others. Especially when there are either too many of "them," or they are "too different" or too easy to ignore. Current events such as the #OscarsSoWhite and #BlackLivesMatter remind us we do not have everyone equally represented on the playing field. Racial inequality, prohibition of gay marriage, sexism and gender inequities, police brutality against minorities, institutional discrimination, immigration challenges, and sanctuary for refugees are not just U.S. issues, but global issues. To believe these issues, do not limit our ability; to be inclusive would be acting like an ostrich with its head in the sand.

Immutable Forces

The three immutable forces that lead to all this confusion and keep us stuck are first dominance, (power and privilege), then unconscious bias, and finally degrees of difference. They cannot be changed; they are omnipresent and perennial. Let's take a brief introductory look at all three before we discuss them in greater detail in Chapters 4 to 6.

Dominance (power and privilege) pervades every situation. In fact, dominance (power and privilege) was a key factor in the anecdotal stories shared earlier in this chapter. Each story was told from the perspective of a member of the dominant culture. They expected things would not change and their world would continue to accommodate the way they expected things to be. Some of their unspoken assumptions or demands were the following:

1. Don't move too many people of difference into my neighborhood.
2. Don't label the food in any other language than mine.
3. Would the last (White) American bring the flag (as there is too much diversity here).
4. We need to move back home (where it is more homogenous).
5. We are not comfortable when there are too many of "them" telling us their stories of discrimination.
6. The neighborhood is changing and we don't like it.

With the exception of #3, where the subject is specific, all of the others could be held by any dominant group anywhere in the world, but it is equally likely your unconscious programming read each of these as if they were told from the U.S. or Anglo perspective.

The point is dominance is everywhere. Dominance is not going away. Over time, the person or group who assumes the role of dominance might change, but the dynamic force of dominance will always be there. Think about your significant relationships. Who is dominant today and has it always been like that? Does that role change on occasions? Is it situation-specific? Who is in charge of the big decisions and who decides where to go for dinner? People move seamlessly in and out of dominance, depending on their role and the perceived status of the situation.

Unconscious bias is the second immutable force. Our inability to catch and manage our blind spots represents a clear and present danger to our ability to be inclusive.

It was 7.30 p.m. on a Friday evening and I was at Dallas/Fort Worth airport waiting to board a flight home to Fort Lauderdale. As I stepped on board, I took with me a couple of unconscious biases I did not know I had. Despite the fact that I had at that time over 2 million air miles I was and still am a nervous flyer, and so, had developed an unconscious habit of looking into the cockpit to check out the pilot. Of course, this was pre 9/11 when the cockpit door was open and you could peer in. As I looked into the cockpit, I was greeted by a woman sitting in the captain's seat. My stomach began to churn. A woman pilot! For a few moments I seriously considered getting off the plane and taking a flight home on Saturday morning. Wait a moment—I am a Diversity consultant, I am not meant to think like this. What is happening? As I processed my feelings, I realized my image of a competent airline pilot was a tall white male with silver hair, who looked like he was ex-Military. Now *he* could fly the plane, I was not sure she could. I stayed on the plane, and she got the plane and me home safely. Our idea of who is competent is often hidden deep inside our unconscious mind, but manifests consciously in the choices we make and the attitudes we adopt. We do not always realize what is influencing our thoughts, feelings, and behaviors and that is particularly true when it comes to our judgment about people.

Degrees of difference is the third immutable force. This immutable force is less obvious, and yet, it has been hidden in plain sight for as long as we have been talking about diversity and inclusion.

All of the corporate efforts to address diversity are focused on large topics or categories, such as gender, sexual orientation, race and culture, generational groups, and differently abled, to name a few. What is not addressed, or indeed fully understood, is just how different people are within each of these groups. You cannot lump everyone together and assume you understand the group.

It goes without saying, men and women are different. Just as it goes without saying, Anglo cultures are different from people of color and people who identify as gay, lesbian, bisexual, and transgender are different. These high-level "categories" have been the focus of our diversity work for many years, but there is not enough granularity and delineation.

Within every group, there are differences that can derail our efforts, and yet are often ignored. You can tell yourself women are women, but that would be delusional. There is a myriad of differences in a group of women and not just because they are all individuals. Women do not necessarily get along with each other, and some of the reasons are based on our perception of each other's difference. Within the LGBTI community, there are differences in the way people perceive each other. There is a color line within communities of color, and even within generational groups, such as Baby Boomers, there are differences in perception. Are you a Boomer who has retired? Or are you a Boomer who has retired on the job, counting the days to actual retirement? Or perhaps you are a Boomer who is busy reinventing yourself and are energized by the thought of "*refirement*" and creating a third wave in your career?

Judgments proliferate when it comes to degrees of difference, and perhaps, the biggest judgment of all is whether you are even willing to identify with the group that others assume you are a member of. Falling on that sword (and many do) has derailing implications for achieving inclusivity. I have spoken to women in senior leadership, who do not want to be identified with the women's group in their organization. I also heard stories from people of color, who distance themselves from their own groups in order to be more acceptable to their White colleagues and managers, or LGBTI employees who not only stay in the closet, but also disassociate from other LGBTI colleagues. Why do these views and behaviors exist and what impact do they have on the individuals concerned and others who bear witness to the withdrawal or rejection? What are we doing to more fully understand these views and beliefs? We cannot resolve the inclusion puzzle if we do not take time to more fully understand the existing complexities of the degrees of difference.

All three of these immutable forces—dominance, unconscious bias, and degrees of difference are here to stay. We need to know they exist, acknowledge they are immutable, accept they have the power to derail our efforts, and figure out ways to make them work for us, and not against us. We will soon see how easily we can get tangled up in these particularly entrenched forces and why it is so challenging to see the inclusion forest from the immutable trees.

CHAPTER 4

The Perennial Presence of Dominance

Dominance is here to stay. There is no such thing as equality in any relationship, whether at home or at work. Someone is always more dominant than the other.

Dominance has been around since the beginning of time. People dominate other people. Bullies excel at dominance, but so do public figures and political candidates among others. Countries dominate other countries and cultural groups within countries dominate other cultural groups. This dynamic is not going to change, but what does change over time is who will be the dominant person or group? As we look at current events, we can see countries becoming dominant in the world economy that were not on the radar screen 25 years ago.

Another reality that will never change is dominance comes packaged with power, privilege, and a sense of entitlement. These three factors become a way of being for dominant people, manifesting in obvious and not so obvious ways that are so fused they can be outside the conscious awareness of the perpetrator. It is hard to believe, but individuals may not actually realize the full impact of their behavior on others. Subculture members are often surprised to find out dominant members do not see the power they have in the same light as them. In reality, these three variables have an impact on both dominant culture and subculture members, and much of it plays out with the implicit consent of both parties.

I grew up in Scotland in a predominantly White Christian community. My father was a member of the local golf club and took my brother and me to learn to play golf. All of the members were predominantly White males. Women were only allowed to play golf on Tuesday mornings and unless accompanied by a male partner on a Sunday afternoon. Children were not allowed into the club house. It all seemed perfectly normal. That was the way the world was. Or, so I thought. By the time I was 18, my feminist self was surfacing, and I began to rail against the idea women could only play on Tuesday mornings. This caused me to give up golf for many years, dismissing it as a male bastion and not somewhere I wanted to be. I did not come back to golf until I was 32, and only then, when a male companion told me I could not beat him. I did, but that is a story for another day.

What I completely failed to notice at the golf club was not the treatment of women, but that there were no other cultures or religions represented. Every member was White and Christian. For me, that was the unquestioning norm. The sin of omission was completely invisible to me. As animated as I became about women, I had no idea we were being exclusionary. I certainly would not have called it White privilege or religious exclusion and yet it was.

Life has moved on from these formative years in Scotland, and throughout my professional life, my eyes and my mind have been opened. I have heard a lot of stories about privilege and the lack of privilege during Diversity and Inclusion workshops, interviews, and focus groups. When we explore the issues of dominance and invisible privilege during a workshop, we ask men to describe the privileges of being a man in the workplace, and men often look at us with blank stares and a shrug of their shoulders, genuinely not sure what we are asking. They never thought about this before as they usually think of themselves as an individual. Part of the challenge here is the members of dominant cultures, whether it is White, male, heterosexual, or able-bodied, tend not to see themselves as group members and do not always realize "others" view them as a group. On more than one occasion, I have heard men say "My name is (John) and I never think of myself as a White male." Dominance allows its members to have the luxury of seeing themselves as individuals. What comes packaged with that is the myopic ability to judge their world based on their own behaviors and not as representative of "a group." Ironically and conversely being equally capable of judging the behavior of one member of another group as a representative of that group.

When we ask the women in workshops what are the privileges of being a woman at work, they tell us they do not have a privilege, but have plenty to say about lack of privilege and the impact of living and working in a male-dominated culture. Many, but not all, tell stories of inequities, including not having their voices heard as credible, not having the same access to major projects, and being labeled as too aggressive if they are outspoken and direct.

When we then ask White people to speak about privileges again, we are often met with puzzled looks as if no one quite understands the question. They shrug their shoulders and look uncomfortable and some-what guilty as they tell us they never really thought about that question before. They do not wake up every day, look in the mirror and say, "oh my goodness, I am still White today." It is just not in their conscious aware-ness. People of color standing on the other side of the room during that exercise often look incredulous, asking themselves, "How can they not know?" Conversely, having privileges does not guarantee that only good things happen for you; it is just that if you are a member of a dominant culture, then societal odds are weighted in your favor.

When we ask people of color about their experience of privilege at work, they shake their heads and tell us they are not seen as the dominant group; they are a minority and they know it. They tell us they do not have a privilege; on the contrary, they tell stories of being the only one in a meeting, or being ignored, passed over for promotions, not trusted, and labeled as lazy or being told they are too aggressive.

When I think about the intersections of the relationship between dominance and subordinance, I am somewhat whimsically reminded of the father figure in *Mary Poppins*, played by David Tomlinson, when he sings "The Life I lead"—"A British Bank is run with precision, a British home requires nothing less. Tradition, discipline, and rules must be the tools … or we will have a ghastly mess." His wife looks on with feigned admiration and tells him how proud she is, while at the same time, rolling her eyes in a knowing manner. The implication of the rolled eyes being she is aware of what is happening and, yet, is complicit in the dance. We are all in this together, albeit tugging on opposite ends of the same rope.

Would it not be simpler to just stop talking about it? Why can we not just see everyone as an individual? Why do we have to talk about this, it only makes matters worse? Why can we not just focus on similarities, and not differences? Why can we not see that things that happen to women and people of color (can) also happen to men and White people? Why is the story so different? Is it really a one-up-one-down situation or is there a level playing field of inequities—things that happen to all of us as humans, which are then filtered unfairly through the lens of whatever diverse group suits the story?

Over the years of doing Diversity and Inclusion work, I have realized all of the privileges I have by being White European, Christian, and heterosexual. It is hard for me to believe that there was ever a time in my life when I simply had no idea. I was completely oblivious to the very inkling of dominance or privilege, as it related to me. It quite simply did not make it onto my personal radar screen.

On the other hand, I have almost always been aware of the societal and workplace challenges of being a member of subcultural groups—for example, being a woman, an immigrant, and recently, more consciously a Baby Boomer. In any given day, I move seamlessly and often without conscious awareness from dominance and privilege into subordinance and assimilation, taking on the appropriate mantle or task to fit the situation.

The presence of dominance (privilege, power, and entitlement) can show up in various ways. Are you always the one talking in a meeting? Do you have a propensity to interrupt or pull the conversation back to you? Do you make your presence felt by being controlling? Do you feel entitled to have things go your way? If any of these apply to you, then there is a high percentage chance you are viewed by others as not only dominating, but also acting out of your invisible privilege.

In direct response to these types of behavior, the party being dominated learns to collude in order to cope and survive. People adjust to the impact of dominance without even realizing they are doing it. We remain silent in meetings. We lose our voice at important times and then talk to others in the hallways about our frustration. We tolerate bullies and then wish we had said something later. We dress better than them to defend against being seen as less than. We wait our turn to speak, instead of jumping in and interrupting, as we see them do. We change what we were about to say midstream when we sense they are uncomfortable with what we are saying. We watch their body language for clues of approval, disapproval, or change in mood. We avoid being in their presence when we can help it. We shrink our aura hoping they will not notice us. We feel relieved to spend time with our own group, so that we can breathe more easily.

I particularly resonate with Derald Wing Sue who calls these exchanges the micro-aggressions of everyday life and suggests the relatively invisible nature of these seemingly insignificant gestures "allows the perpetrator to continue in the belief of their innocence" (Sue 2010). Sue goes on to explain that even when these micro-aggressions become visible, they are seen as insignificant or small events. It is not the one-off experience that catches our attention; it is the consistency of these occurrences when they begin to form a pattern. The catch-22 being if the individual points them out they are minimized with statements such as "You are being over-sensitive" or "These things happen to me too" and yet ignoring them pretty much guarantees the behavior(s) will continue. I return to my theory on patterns; when it happens once, it is an accident; when it happens twice, it is a coincidence; and three times, it becomes a pattern. The impact of patterns, however, is like water dripping on a stone, and the consistency of that is de-energizing and disempowering.

I was very pleased and proud when one of my former consultants, Alan Johnson, wrote a book about privilege, which also highlights these micro-aggressions. In *Privilege, Power and Difference*, Alan speaks of how privilege can be as simple as whether we look at someone or look away. Whether we welcome them with a smile or a stare. Whether we avoid touching their skin when giving or taking something from them, and how closely we watch them to see what they are up to. These seemingly subtle gestures are most likely to be noticed by the person experiencing them, and not necessarily by the person perpetrating them (Johnson 2001).

There is a view that we should stop talking about diversity and just all get along as human beings. Of course, that is not realistic, and it is certainly not what is happening. I recently heard a cable television news anchor saying we needed to arrive at the day when race in America does not matter and we do not see color. That day will never arrive. Where we need to arrive is at a place where we do see race and color; and they do not make us uncomfortable because we have made space for each other and respect our differences. The angst being created between the current U.S. movement "Black Lives Matter" and the push by the U.S. dominant culture groups to say "All Lives Matter" is part of the same issue of invisible privilege and subculture experiences. It may be prima facie hard to argue with the concept that all lives matter, but what is not being understood by the proponents of the "All Lives Matter" message is if we accept that slogan as our mantra we are effectively saying to people of color we want to maintain the status quo—where in reality Black lives matter less and racial discrimination, police brutality, incarceration, and so on will continue.

The point being missed here is a big one; in fact, it is huge. We can only reach a place where *all lives matter* when the dominant culture, namely White, have done the work it takes to listen, to understand, and to accept that there really can be a difference in the way people are treated based on race and economic status. De facto, accepting there is a valid reason behind the "Black Lives Matter" movement, people of color will not trust the members of the White culture(s) until they believe we heard them. Incidents such as the one in Flint, Michigan (a predominantly African American community), provide a recent example of the inequity of treatment. The decisions made by the local government officials caused the water to become toxic, causing lead poisoning and serious health problems for everyone living there, including children and pregnant mothers. The questions this raised are valid. Was this allowed to happen because the city is predominantly Black and poor? And conversely, would it have been allowed to happen if the city had been White and affluent?

I watched an interview recently where one of the leaders from the *Black Lives Matter* movement explained that if the meeting were in support of a cure for breast cancer, you would not expect someone to stand up and say, "Wait a minute, prostate cancer matters as well." Everyone understands breast cancer is an important and life-threatening issue. Telling African Americans to stop saying Black Lives Matter is like telling them we do not accept their point of view; we do not think there is a need to rid ourselves of the cancer of racism, police brutality, excessive incarceration of young Black men, and institutionalized racism toward the Black communities. If we refuse to listen, if we are quick to dismiss, and profess to not understand the perspectives from another diverse group or if we refuse to understand they even have a story, then they have no reason to trust us, and we can never move to an agreement that all lives matter. We can only get there when we all step up and accept responsibility to work together to get rid of the cancer. Then and only then can we say with impunity that all lives matter.

These issues are not unique to the United States as there is racism and a hierarchy of cultural biases in every country. To name a few, Australia faces challenges with the relationship between Anglo-Australians and Indigenous Australians; every country in Europe is facing a migrant/refugee situation of gargantuan proportions, and within each country in Asia, there are not only cultural hierarchies, but there is also a dynamic tension between expats and locals.

A healthy solution will require that the dominant culture members are willing to lean in and understand the presence and dynamics of dominance and own responsibility for change. Facing up to the reality of privilege and entitlement will take us in the right direction, but are we ready to do that?

Plugging the Energy Drain

Dominance can be both energizing and enervating for the same person depending on where they are standing on the continuum at any given time and which of their facets or social identity groups are central to the presenting situation. As we have multiple social identities, many of us move in and out of dominance on a daily basis and our experience is dictated by our socially constructed stories, our frame of reference, our social identity group(s), and our life experiences. If you are an African American, heterosexual, male you will experience an invisible privilege by being heterosexual and male, but may experience lack of privilege based on being a Black male in the United States.

When I am living in the dominance and privilege of being British and surrounded by people from my own culture, I breathe easier. We laugh at the same jokes. We can talk in shorthand and we don't have to think much about what we mean. British people tend to have quite a dry sense of humor, and we often tease each other with an edge of sarcasm that might cause outsiders to raise their eyebrows.

When I find myself focused on any of my subordinate roles, there is more tension in my body. I am more aware of what people say, especially if it is not diversity-sensitive, I don't always find the throwaway jokes funny, and I might metaphorically raise my eyebrows a little more often. Negative comments about women, even when said jokingly, can set my teeth on edge. My subordinate roles cause me to unconsciously remain "on guard." Dominance and subordinance are intrinsic to human social relationships and are so embedded in our patterns of behavior that most people do not even notice the shifts they make to accommodate the duality of their roles.

A further complicating factor is I can never let my guard down as the subordinance role is always lurking close by, and my body is fine-tuned to be on alert as these issues can arise at any time, even when I am in the presence of people from my own British culture. This forces me to need to move seamlessly from breathing easily to holding my breath as I instinctively manage my feelings and reactions to both dominant and subordinate situations.

As if it were not convoluted enough, it is not merely self-perceptions that matter. It is the perceptions and labels others place on us that play a role in the health of our diverse relationships. The labels we are consciously and unconsciously assigned by others and the assumptions they project also have a direct impact on how we are treated and how we respond. I know people who look White, but are actually Latino or Black, and they tell stories of people saying things to them about other groups because they are assumed to be White. A consulting colleague of mine is Japanese, and during the Rodney King riots in Los Angeles, she stayed indoors for days because she knew if she went out, she would be assumed to be Korean. Asian participants in our workshops often tell stories of being asked where they are from. When they say "California," they are asked a follow up question "No, where are you really from?" And then "Well, where are your parents from?" If the answer remains California, the questioner looks confused as that is clearly not the answer they were looking for.

Dominance and subordinance are opposite sides of the same coin. For dominance to exist, subordinance must be its "kissing cousin." While the coin only has two sides, namely, dominance and subordinance, each face of the coin should also have a Janus figurehead on it, because you have to be conscious of looking in both directions. First of all, how you perceive your own dominance and subordinance and then examine how others perceive it?

Let's explore that further by giving each side of the coin a Part A and Part B.

As you know, part of my dominant cultural identity is White and heterosexuals, and my subcultural groups are women, immigrants, and Baby Boomers.

1A: Dominance—My Perception of My Dominance

I must be able to understand how I think about myself as a member of a dominant culture. For example, how do I perceive myself as a White person? Am I aware of having privilege and of how my privilege benefits me? For instance, being White gives me access to places, such as my golf club, without a question or raised eyebrows and a "What is she doing here?" ambience; in fact, having a Scottish accent is a distinct advantage when you want to play golf as all kinds of assumptions are made about your love of the game. I am more likely than comparable people of color to be approved for a loan at the bank, and I can choose to ignore or acknowledge my racial identity. I can regard myself as just simply an individual and a human being. Some of my privileges were mirrored back to me when a few years ago, I traveled frequently with people of color as we were co-facilitating Diversity workshops. I noticed that when we went out for dinner, we were often given a table near the kitchen, near the door, or near the bathrooms. I also witnessed an incident when my African American consulting colleague put his bag in the overhead bin in the first class and the flight attendant told him, "Sir, these overhead bins are reserved for first class passengers." He was actually in first class, but the assumption was he was not.

What about the unspoken privileges of being heterosexual—what is it I take for granted? I am free to reveal my sexual orientation without fear of judgment. I do not need to worry or wonder whether my sexual orientation is being used against me in a promotion decision. I can put pictures of my partner on my desk at work and not worry about being judged because of his sexual orientation. I can talk freely about where we went on vacation and hold hands in public without people noticing or pointing it out. My identity is not reduced to my sexual orientation, and I see evidence that being heterosexual is the approved norm everywhere I look.

1B: Dominance—Perception by Others of My Dominance

I should be aware and concerned about how I am impacting other people because of my dominance as a White, heterosexual person, and how they perceive me (not as an individual, but as a representative of these diverse groups). The first blind spot here is I will often not notice that I am being seen by non-White group members as "acting White or entitled" or being viewed by members of the LGBTI community as being presumptuously heterosexual. I was at my home airport last week, standing at baggage claim, when my African American limo driver arrived and a White woman came up to him and asked if he would lift her bags off the baggage ramp and take them outside. She assumed he was an airport porter; although he was not wearing the airport uniform. The driver declined and rolled his eyes at me as if to say that is not the first time I was mistaken for the porter. The assumption of privilege is to see people of color in subordinate roles. A number of years ago, I was checking into a hotel and made the same mistake. I turned around looking for the bellman to take my bags to my room and saw an African American man behind me. He looked startled and bemused as he declined to take my bags and politely pointed out he was a fellow guest who was also checking in.

2A: Subordinance—My Perception of My Subordinance

How do I perceive myself as a member of subcultural groups? As a woman, a Baby Boomer, or as an immigrant, what behaviors do I adjust in order to fit in? What do I hide or cover up in order to be more acceptable to the dominant culture? Women intuitively learn that if they are too meek and timid, we are told we lack gravitas and presence; but, if we are too strong, we are assigned another label. I am acutely aware that over the years, there were times I remained silent and withheld my opinion because I either did not feel safe as a woman to speak up or because I felt my point of view would not be welcomed or understood. No one told me to do that; no one said my views were not welcome. That is a story I told myself because I was sitting in the middle of my socially conditioned subordinance at the time. I am also aware I will wait my turn to speak rather than jumping into the conversation, if I feel I am in the presence of men with status and power. As a young and inexperienced facilitator, I once took the risk of telling a group of men they were joking around and not taking the subject matter seriously and was penalized for that intervention by their collective lack of cooperation for the rest of the workshop. As a result, it affected my behavior for many years, as my unconscious reaction was to lose my voice and remain silent and anxious when in similar situations.

2B: Subordinance—Perception by Others of My Subordinance

How do other people perceive me, not as an individual, but as a representative of my diverse group(s)? This is a particularly a complicated sector as I am dealing with how I am perceived by the members of my own groups (women and immigrants) and how the dominant cultural groups perceive me (men and naturalized citizens).

I have lived in the United States since 1980 and I am a U.S. citizen. When I became a citizen, a few people sat me down and took it upon themselves to tell me how I should vote and explain how things are done in America. This happened despite that I have lived here for many years and am well aware of how things are done here. Not to mention, I thought voting was a private affair and an inalienable right of citizenship. My reaction was to quietly ignore them. After all, trying to push back would just have earned me another label.

Subculture dynamics come into play whenever people view you as less than they are. I am always on alert when dealing with tradesmen who come to fix something at my home. My ear is fine-tuned for evidence they are implying that as a woman, I don't know enough to understand or being patronizing enough to ask where my husband is and naïve enough to believe they can overprice the job and still seal the deal. Being constantly on guard is exhausting, de-energizing, and demeaning. It is not the "unbearable lightness of being" that drives us on those occasions; it is the "exhausting weight of knowing." There it is again, more water dripping on a stone and more collusion. It can leave you feeling powerless and exhausted.

The Power of the Weak

It is an interesting phenomenon that the subculture members always know more about dominant culture(s) than the dominant culture(s) know about themselves or the subcultures. That is a bit of a tongue-twister, but fundamentally, what I am saying is if you are, for example, gay or lesbian, in order to survive in a predominantly heterosexual culture, you need to know and understand the nuances of the heterosexual culture. You need to know what they value, how they think about themselves, and what they think about your group. You need to figure out what you must do to fit in and not make them too uncomfortable. Additionally, you need to know and understand your own cultural group. If you are heterosexual, you can in fact live your entire life never having to think about the gay or lesbian community, far less try to understand what the LGBTI culture really cares about. The same is true for all other dominant groups. White people do not need to spend time in predominantly Black, Latino, or Asian communities and able-bodied, people do not need to know and understand the challenges for the differently abled unless they have a personal reason to do so. Peggy McIntosh, the woman who actually coined the phrase "White Privilege," points out in her now classic article how much we take for granted when we are members of a dominant culture. She highlights a significant number of invisible privileges, including the fact that White people can see themselves reflected on television and marketing ads in a positive light, can play with dolls that look like them, buy

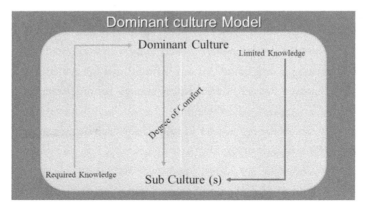

greeting cards that speak to them, and use flesh-colored Band-Aids to match their skin (McIntosh 1988).

All of this might have us ask if people in the subcultural groups are powerless in the one-up-one-down relationship, but that is not the case. Some of the coping mechanisms allow people to take control of the situation. Solutions range from ensuring you work harder than everyone else to prove you deserve a seat at the table, dressing better than the mainstream to send the message you have status, agreeing to some extent to go along to get along, adjusting your style when you are in the presence of dominance to ensure you still "fit in," and assimilating to the culture on the basis that if you are not present your voice will be missing as in the recent debate about the Oscars not nominating more actors of color (#SoWhiteOscars). To boycott or to attend, that is the question? Opting out is not an option, and that leaves the only option being how to stay in the relationship and cause change from the inside out.

Can We Give Dominance a Facelift?

Given its many faces and immutable nature, what can we do to mitigate the impact of dominance on inclusion?

The omnipresent reality of dominance is foundational to why we talk about diversity and inclusion. It is the relationship of dominance to subordinance that has all of us, including dominant culture members, adjusting our style, and on many occasions, being politically correct or covering who we really are. It is an energy drain, a productivity detractor, and a damper on our ability to be creative and innovative. Yet, it is an immutable force and not going away. It is without question a business imperative to address these complex issues, and in doing so, strive to gain the return on investment (ROI) and improve the bottom line.

As dominance is inevitable, the most critical thing to do is to help both dominant and subculture members become more aware of the power dynamics it creates. As we have seen, dominant culture members make assumptions of privilege and entitlement, and subculture members are constantly adjusting their style to assimilate and fit in with the dominant culture. Raising this to consciousness by awareness, ownership, and minimization are the keys.

By becoming more aware, it is possible for dominant members to behave more inclusively and for subculture members to consciously limit their assimilation behaviors and be freed up to bring more creative and innovative energy to the relationship. Minimizing or limiting the number of times we act out of our privilege or give in to assimilation behaviors will benefit the growth of our inclusion skills. Being able to talk honestly and courageously about this dynamic will also help to defang the snake and limit its power.

Of course, there is still one spanner in the works because all of these suggestions assume good intent and willingness on the part of the dominant culture. Having power and privilege is pretty seductive, and the thought of giving it up is not appealing. If there is fear of losing ground, losing territory, losing status, or losing control, then there will be resistance to allowing change, cooperation, and collaboration to happen. That is in large part why this is an immutable force. In the interests of inclusivity are we willing to moderate our dominance?

References

Johnson, A.G. 2001. *Privilege, Power and Difference.* Boston, MA: McGraw Hill Publishers.

McIntosh, P. 1988. "White Privilege and Male Privilege." Center for Research on Women Working paper Series, No. 189: 19.

Sue, D.W. 2010. *Micro-Aggressions in Everyday Life: Race, Gender and Sexual Orientation.* Hoboken, NJ: John Wiley and Sons.

CHAPTER 5

Bumping in to Our Blind Spots

It was 30 years ago, but I remember it as if it was yesterday.

It was a cold January day, and I was in Chicago on business. My flight had been delayed and I had just checked into my hotel. I had a late afternoon client meeting and needed to iron the outfit I wanted to wear. In 1986, they did not supply an iron and ironing table in every room, so I called the housekeeping and requested an iron be sent to my room. Forty-five minutes and four phone calls later the iron had still not arrived. The woman I had spoken to on each occasion did not speak English very well and had a distinct and difficult-to-understand accent. This was only adding to my frustration as I felt perhaps she had not picked up the urgency of my request. After the fifth call, there was a knock on my hotel room door. I took a couple of determined strides toward the door. I was intent on telling the housekeeper what I thought about the delay. When I opened the door all I actually said was, "Thank you very much." As I closed the door and stood with the iron in my hands, I asked myself, "What just happened?"

What had just happened was that the woman on the other side of the door did not fit the profile I had in my head. Instead she closely resembled *my* grandmother. I realized in that moment I was willing to be strident and less than polite to someone else's grandmother, but not to *my* own. That realization stopped me in my tracks. Are you kidding me! I am a Diversity Consultant. What was I thinking?

This incident was a huge life lesson on the power of unconscious bias. I was a relatively new Diversity Consultant and took pride in knowing I valued diversity and was able to help others to see why we needed to be more aware and more inclusive. And yet, here I was willing to berate a woman not only because my iron was late, but apparently because she came from another culture. When confronted with a replica of my White grandmother, my indignation dissipated, and I became polite and appreciative. What was that about? Where did that mind virus come from? The incident made me realize no one gets to be a phenomenological exception, not even me. Doing this work does not give you a free pass. We are products of our environment and the cutural messages, unconscious biases, and blind spots run deep. We all have them; no exceptions.

That was 30 years ago and it happened to me again this morning—I bumped into another blind spot. Well, actually it is the same blind spot that had me select a male airline pilot as being more competent than a woman pilot. I have recently sustained some water damage to part of my wood flooring at home and needed a professional to come and look at it. I was referred to a company who are experts in flooring, and the owner called me to arrange for someone to come on Monday to look at the damage. During the call, he said, "Claudia will be there on Monday" and my inner voice went into overdrive. What! He is sending a woman to look at my wood flooring. It turns out he meant Claudio, but my initial knee jerk reaction was a woman could not possibly know how to fix my flooring. In these moments, I am reminded no matter how much work we do and how much awareness we have, the immutable force of unconscious bias does not go away; we must learn to catch it. I do not think I am alone in having gender roles unconsciously fused tightly to specific genders. What roles do you assign definitively to women or men? What is your reaction when you are confronted with the opposite gender fulfilling a role you did not anticipate when your mental model was expecting someone else?

A Conscious Disclaimer

Put the brain down and walk away!

The first rule of public speaking is to never tell your audience you are afraid, or you are the substitute speaker, or you are not as knowledgeable as the person who spoke before you. So why am I about to break that rule?

I am not a neuroscientist or an expert on the brain. I am probably in the eyes of neuroscientists one of those consultants they disparagingly talk about as pseudoscientists. It is true that a little knowledge can be a dangerous thing, so what makes me think I cannot only write an entire chapter on unconscious bias, but also speak about it globally in keynotes and workshops. What insights do I have to offer you that you cannot find out yourself just by stirring up the Google juices?

You have most likely heard the old adage that you do not pay a carpenter for how many nails she hammers; you pay her for knowing where to hammer and how hard to hit the nail. When I combine my depth of knowledge of the diversity and inclusion journey with years of rich research data generated globally from focus groups, workshops, interviews, and results from my Unconscious Bias and Inclusion assessments, I see patterns and stories that are not only compelling and worth sharing, but inextricably connected to our unconscious biases. Leaders need insights to drive results. They value measurements and numbers that can definitively prove the business case and motivate their people to take action. I have a proven track record on delivering compelling measurements where clients win high profile awards as a result of the progress they can make. So, I respectfully ask that you cut me some slack on the neuroscience track and come with me if you dare into the inner vaults of the Diversity and Inclusion "mind-field."

The Real Tip of the Iceberg

A couple of years ago, I was in a grocery store and asked the bakery assistant for six bagels. She replied, "Oh, you sound so intelligent." I am sure you will agree that you don't have to be really smart to ask for six bagels.

I realized what she had done was to act out of one of her unconscious biases and project intelligence on to my British accent. While it made me smile, it also made me wonder what level of intelligence she would unconsciously project on to others if their accent was less pleasing to her ear. Again, I was reminded of the hidden privileges of being perceived as a member of the dominant culture. Assumptions and projections are all part of the unconscious biases that add to the complexity of inclusion.

Freud said the conscious mind was the tip of the iceberg, but in later years, other psychologists have said that Freud was wrong and that the conscious mind is a snowball on top of the tip of the iceberg and everything else is the subconscious mind. Neuroscientists today would agree that most of our sophisticated high-level thinking is left to the unconscious mind. Have you ever completed a task and then wondered how that happened as you do not recall being consciously present during the process? Pilots put commercial jets on auto-pilot, and in many ways, our brain operates on auto-pilot without us consciously realizing what is driving our decisions. With the enormity of that image, it would be helpful if we could develop mental red alerts to warn us when our unconscious biases are driving our decisions?

The challenge here is once again we need to be able to raise these biases to a conscious level—move them from the back of our neck to the edge of our shoulder where they are, at least in our peripheral vision. It is a bit like having Jiminy Cricket on your shoulder tapping you on the side of the head and reminding you that you are about to be influenced by a bias.

I am impressed by the new feature recently installed in many cars where a red triangle on the wing mirrors warns you when you have a car in your blind spot. It would be wonderful to have red triangles hovering over our shoulders to alert us to our inclusion blind spots. I wish it were that simple. Perhaps, that is not possible, but we can invoke a series of mental red alerts. It is possible to become more mindful. Slow down your decision-making process to allow yourself time to reflect before putting your mouth in gear too quickly and jumping into that biased decision.

A few years ago I was working with a client and his audio-visual technician to set up a workshop. I was introduced to the technician as Dr. Turnbull, and we all worked together for about 20 minutes on the setup with my laptop and the client's projector and equipment. My client then told the technician, "Dr. Turnbull needs a microphone" to which the technician replied, "I will get it for *him* when *he* arrives." I am not sure whose jaw dropped faster, mine or my client's.

When we unconsciously have mental models of appropriate gender roles, as I did in my earlier examples, this is another illustration of the power of unconscious bias and the complexity of inclusion. If the audio-visual technician had slowed down his mental processes and been more mindful of the situation, perhaps, he would have become more consciously aware that he was already speaking to the presenter. His unconscious mind and mental maps leapt out in front of his conscious awareness.

Unconscious Bias and Inclusion

It seems remarkable that anyone in the 21st century would think it was OK to tell a woman that she has "Bitchy Resting Face" or "Resting Bitch Face." And yet, it has become a commonly used term to describe women who have a negative look on their face. This label and its consequences are loaded with both conscious and unconscious bias and the flawed belief that it is a uniquely female characteristic is biased in itself.

Just the very word "bitch" makes you associate this term with women, and not in a good way. The word "bitch" does not have any positive conations unless you are talking factually about a female dog. Scientific research on resting bitch face (RBF) syndrome, however, does not support the use of this label specifically for women as *both* men and women can have "resting bitch face." The research explored facial expressions for 100,000 people and concluded that RBF applies to both genders and is an indicator of contempt. There are 500 different facial muscles and when 97 percent of them are at rest you look relaxed, but when only 94 percent are at rest the other three percent show contempt. Having one side of your mouth turned down, your eyes slightly closed, and/ or your head tilted off to the side are all indicators of skepticism and/ or contempt. A speaker colleague of mine, Dr. Louise Mahler (Mahler 2016), an expert in communications, spoke on this subject with the Australian media recently and explained recent research demonstrates when men use RBF they are viewed to be 10 percent *more* competent, but when women use RBF, they are viewed as 14 percent *less* competent. The good news for both genders is RBF is a learned behavior you can teach yourself not to do it, but given the unconscious benefits to men and the negative projections on women I am persuaded that women should break the habit first.

If you Google "how many unconscious biases exist," you will find a list of nearly 200 (https://en.wikipedia.org/wiki/List_of_cognitive_biases).

My somewhat whimsical favorite is "the IKEA effect" described as a tendency to place a disproportionately high value on the objects you partially assemble yourself, regardless of the quality of the end result, which may explain our fascination with ourselves.

It would be reasonable to expect in the 21st century we should have solved these issues, at least in the workplace if not in society, and yet, we have not. I have interviewed many managers and employees across different global geographies and industrial sectors to discuss their views on diversity and inclusion. Most of these interviews went well and were incredibly professional and supportive with many male champions of change stepping up. But some stand out in my mind *not* for their support but for the inappropriate and confronting things that were said. These incidents remind me while we focus on unconscious bias; conscious bias has not gone away. They are also a reminder of why it is so emotionally exhausting to lean in to diversity and inclusion and why we cannot let our guard down. I vividly recall two show-stopping conversations that left me wondering if things were being said just for the shock and awe effect. One manager told me, he thought efforts to promote diversity had gone too far and his organization needed to "get rid of these people who have grown balls." The second manager told me, he was in the process of interviewing for an opening in his department and the guys on his team told him to be sure and hire someone who had "wobbly bits." These comments were made while simultaneously putting on a professional face to the employees and other leaders implying support for the company's diversity efforts. In reality, you can hide all you like, but people see you anyway. When we do not sincerely support something employees know it. There is "leakage" and our real attitude bleeds out in some ways. They manifest in our body language RBF and in our throwaway comments and lack of enthusiasm for Diversity programs and initiatives. Our unconscious biases show up and give the game away.

Unconscious bias does not only live in our minds, it also lives in our body memory. I was raised as a Protestant at the Church of Scotland. We had one Catholic Church in town and one Catholic school. I distinctly remember being afraid of them. The children from the Catholic school walked to school on the other side of the street from us and wore different uniforms. Their uniforms were navy blue and gray and seemed drab in contrast to our uniforms that were dark green with a red fashionable stripe and seemed far more trendy and cool.

My dad used to say that we only ate fish on Friday as that was the day the Catholics ate fish. That story made them seem strange to me, despite the fact that what dad was really saying was that fish was going to be really fresh on that day. The fact that I heard children at school refer to Catholics as Fenians might have been the mind virus that planted the seeds of disdain and distrust. The word Fenians started its life as an Irish word to describe warriors, but eventually became used as a derogatory label to describe Irish Catholics and then later to describe all Catholics.

I loved to swim and in summer months, I would walk every day after school from our home to the local swimming pool. To get there, I had to pass the Catholic Church. I always made sure to walk on the other side of the street, and when I got level with the main doors to the church, I would turn my head to the left to avoid even a glance in its direction. I am not sure to this day what I thought would happen if I actually looked inside. Perhaps, I thought I would be whisked in and forced to go to confessions, a practice my teenage mind found scary and bizarre. We certainly did not do that at our church.

Thirty years later, I returned to Scotland on vacation with my then significant other and visited my home town. We were driving along Cadzow Street, and as the car came level with the Catholic Church, my head automatically jerked to the left. I was totally stunned. It was not on my conscious mind that we were about to pass the church, and I had long since overcome my nonsensical belief system and fear of Catholics, but nevertheless, my body memory had not. I was in disbelief that a habit from 30 years ago could revisit me without provocation or warning.

The brain loves to habituate, and old habits are hard to break. I recently decided to test my habitual tendencies by moving the knives, forks, and spoons in my cutlery drawer into different slots. Four months later, my hand still goes automatically to where the spoons used to be. Have you ever driven to work and wondered how you got there as you do not remember the journey? We do a lot of things on automatic pilot, including making snap judgments about other people based on old programming and body memories.

I have always been an anxious flyer. Today, I have over five million air miles and travel all over the world on business, so for practical reasons, I had to consciously get over my anxiety. When I first began flying, I used to cross my fingers as the plane was taking off and landing. I have no idea what I thought that was going to do to keep the plane safe or help the pilots be more competent, but it became a habit. In fact, it has become so habitual that years later, I can look down at my hands when we are ascending or descending through 10,000 feet and notice that my fingers are crossed, despite not consciously being aware of doing it. Apparently, my conscious brain thinks I am cool, but my body memory remembers that I am not.

The top two biases that most deeply impact diversity and inclusion are *affinity bias* and *assimilation bias*. They are so important, in fact, that I dedicate an entire chapter to each of them later in the book. The reason they are important is because between the two of them, they capture a significant portion of the unconscious practices that keep us from being more inclusive and equitable in our treatment of difference. Affinity bias is our predilection to be more comfortable surrounding ourselves with people who make us comfortable, people who are more like us than different; perhaps, they went to the same school or at least share much of the same values and beliefs. Assimilation bias is a direct result of the presence of dominance and is a coping mechanism that is unconsciously utilized by subcultural members to fit in with the dominant culture. An example is when a woman tries too hard to act like men by being tough or using profanities to attempt to be "one of the boys." For now, I would like to introduce a few other biases that can also directly influence the diversity and inclusion journey.

Confirmation bias is the tendency to seek out information confirming what we already believe or to discount, downplay, or ignore information that does not agree with our beliefs (Kolodziej 2015). Confirmation bias can really get in the way when we are hiring people or looking to promote them as we seek to confirm from our mental models about who is a good fit for the job and who cannot do the job. During my workshops, I sometimes show the participants photographs of diverse individuals and ask them to make up a quick story about them. One of those pictures is of an older man dressed in a leather jacket, sporting a bandana and a very scruffy white beard. He visibly looks like a biker. The group generally says they would not hire him as he does not fit the image of a corporate manager or executive. Everyone agrees, but on one occasion, a senior manager told us a story about a man, who looked like this individual, who walked into a conference hall where 200 blue-suited executives were waiting for the keynote speaker. He had a yellow Mohawk haircut, blue jeans, and a black tee shirt and clearly did not look as if he belonged to this executive gathering. Silence fell over the room as people looked at each other with puzzled glances. It turned out the individual was not only the keynote speaker, but was the brains behind one of the company's newest and most successful product lines. In that moment, everyone's impression changed from "Hey mate, you are in the wrong room" to him being allowed to be idiosyncratically different. If we constantly deal into our historical mental models, we will be unwilling to take a risk on people who are different. Confirmation bias plays right into the hands of affinity bias and our tendency to hire in our own image.

Halo and horns effect is the tendency for us to attribute behaviors based on past experiences and to project something based on a past memory and not be willing to let go. I recall a senior leader telling me the story of a new employee who during the first three months of employment always arrived early and left work late. A year or so later, his management team complained the individual in question was not committed to his job and was always arriving late. The senior manager said he had a very hard time believing them as he had already applied the halo effect and had unconsciously imprinted a mental image of the young man being very dedicated. He found it hard to let go of that image.

In-group bias is the tendency to give preferential treatment to others perceived to be members of our own group. It is also the propensity to close ranks on people we feel are not part of our in-group. We have all had experiences of feeling we are part of a group and experiences where we knew we were not being made to feel welcome. In fact, we are so territorial that even in a half-day training program, once people sit down at a table and establish their small group, you are often met with a loud groan when you ask people to switch tables. This bias plays out in a myriad of ways from the seemingly insignificant to intractable cultural rules of inclusion. There are 160 million Dalits, or untouchables, who are members of the Hindu caste system in India and are considered to be outcasts. They experience grave discrimination and reprisals if they forget their place (O'Neill 2003). I recall speaking with an Indian woman, who was a consulting colleague, and she told me if an untouchable walked into the room, she would know immediately and would not look at that person; in fact, she might leave the room. In the United Kingdom, social class is a huge issue, and while it does not have the same severe ramifications, everyone intuitively knows their place in society. We can tell by the way you dress and behave if you are Royalty, upper class, middle class, or lower-middle class, or working class. You can really be made to feel you do not belong if you find yourself trying to mix in the wrong circles. The musicals *My Fair Lady* and *Mary Poppins*, albeit in a light-hearted manner, exemplify the British system of social class.

Negativity effect is defined as the tendency when evaluating the cause of behaviors of a person we dislike, to attribute their positive behaviors to the environment and their negative behaviors to their inherent nature (Kolodziej 2015). Have you ever caught yourself doing that? A consulting colleague told me a few years ago about having had the misfortune of working with a woman whom she described as "a pathological sociopath and a stranger to the truth." She regaled me regularly with horror stories of the woman's professional lies and exaggerations. On one occasion, I asked her what redeeming qualities she thought the woman had. She thought for a while and begrudgingly said, "Well, she is an aggressive sales person, but then again the market is hungry for the product she is currently selling." This bias plays out when we want to cognitively rationalize why we should not hire, promote, or interact with someone because our instinct is to not like them, regardless of their skills and talents. We minimize the good and inflate the bad. This bias also plays a role when we are judging people from other diverse groups. If their differences make us uncomfortable, we may be unable to see their skills and talents because our blind spots are blocking our vision.

Pattern recognition bias is a cognitive process that matches memory information with a stimulus in the present. We look for and see patterns sometimes where they don't exist. I am programmed to look for and see evidence of sexism, racism, and every other "ism" related to diversity and inclusion. I hear conversations, and they unconsciously get filtered through my professional lens of unconscious bias. I recall attending a meeting where three speakers were scheduled. Due to traffic problems, the meeting started 30 minutes late. The first speaker was a White male, and he took a determined stance and told the group that despite starting late, he was still going to take his allotted time. The second speaker was a White woman who did not announce it, yet nevertheless, still took her full time causing us to break for lunch 30 minutes late. The afternoon speaker was a man of color who was asked by the organizers to cut his time short and was rushed off the platform at the end of the afternoon. Pattern-recognizing this as a combination of White privilege and unconscious racism, I was indignant on his behalf. I raised the issue with the organizers later and approached the speaker to offer my apologies. The organizers defended their position and said they were only managing the time, and the speaker told me he was fine and had not interpreted it as racism. Sometimes, pattern recognition can get you in a little bit of trouble, especially when you jump in with both feet to rescue people who did not ask to be rescued.

Status quo bias is the tendency to resist change and want to maintain the status quo. This bias plays out with all of our efforts to be more inclusive of diversity. The more we change, the more we want to remain the same. Are you OK with the groceries in your favorite grocery store being labeled in two languages? We really want to embrace differences, but we hold on pretty tight to the way we like things to be. Do you embrace change? Do you celebrate differences? Do you really want everyone around you speaking another language? Do you find yourself wondering if it is possible to stem the tide, slow it down, and just opt for a little bit of diversity?

Stereotyping is a category of bias we all know well. It is the tendency to expect a member of a group to have certain characteristics we attribute to the group without necessarily knowing anything about the individual. An example would be expecting all tall Black men to be able to play basketball or expecting all Asians to be good at math. Another example of stereotyping is when members of a diverse group stand out because of their differences and we proclaim we are weary of seeing them. As you know by now, I am a golfer and a golf fan, but I also like to watch Wimbledon. In recent years, I have heard more than a few people on both sides of the Atlantic say that they are tired of seeing the Williams sisters winning and would really like to see some new players take over. Over the years, I cannot recall anyone saying they were tired of seeing Billie Jean King, Chris Evert, Roger Federer, Rafael Nadal, Pete Sampras, Andre Agassi, or John McEnroe winning.

The difficult truth about unconscious bias is it is an immutable force and is not going away, no matter how much we learn about it. Our unconscious biases show up in micro-seconds and influence our decisions without our conscious awareness. Unconscious bias is an equal opportunity player. It does not respect race, gender, sexual orientation, religion, age, differently abled, status, professional boundaries, social class, or income levels. We all have it. We have no idea how many mental maps and mind viruses are hidden in our subconscious waiting to jump into action. Our brain lays down superconductors for patterns it sees. It makes connections and creates neural pathways. Seeing names, photographs, accents, and places triggers the stored patterns and causes us to show our bias for or against that individual based on these memes or mind viruses. If, for example, you experience older people as not being technically competent, your brain looks for that pattern and immediately helps you make that judgment. Neuroscientists have found our brain is hard-wired to categorize people into groups, filed according to our likes and dislikes, preferences, and biases. I have found this to be true. It is crystal clear to me that even though I objectively and professionally support women, I, nevertheless, have some unconsciously hard-wired mind viruses when it comes to which gender I see as suitable for traditionally male-dominated roles.

In that regard remember my story in Chapter 3 about the flight from Dallas/Fort Worth and my reaction to the female pilot? Fifteen years later, I was on a flight from Canberra to Sydney, Australia. It was a small commuter flight, and the flight attendant was in the aisle serving orange juice, coffee, and biscuits, when I heard a woman's voice come over the intercom. "Good afternoon ladies and gentlemen. We are at 27,000 ft. and will be making our descent into Sydney in 30 minutes. I hope you have enjoyed your flight and thank you for flying with us today." I looked up at the flight attendant and was surprised to see her mouth was not moving. It took me a few seconds to recalibrate to the fact that it was not her making the announcement, and I suddenly realized there must be a woman pilot and I forgot to check. As we were at 27,000 ft., I was not exercising the option to get off the plane. This time, I caught my bias almost as quickly as it leapt to my frontal lobes. I was able to short-circuit my reaction because I was aware of it. This is once again evidence that our unconscious biases do not leave us. As individuals, we need to remain vigilant and mindful. We should then be able to see the bias perched on our shoulder hovering within our peripheral vision. At that stage, we can catch it, hit the pause button, and take a step back before launching into action. It is also important at an organizational level to not only educate people about unconscious bias and its impact, but to be able to name the biases. Here are a few questions to ponder as you reflect on what biases most frequently find their way onto your peripheral vision.

- How do you know that you are really being objective?
- Who is in your in-group?
- Who do you *not* notice at work?
- Who are you conscious of avoiding or ignoring in meetings?
- How do you know when someone is a "good fit?" What criteria are you using?
- What do you mean when you say "we have a meritocracy?"
- How can you be sure there is a meritocracy?
- How do your blind spots impact the quality of your day-to-day decisions?
- How do your personal biases impact your ability to be inclusive?

Overcoming our unconscious biases can leave you feeling like a hamster on a wheel, constantly having to revisit the same situations. Will it ever improve? Unconscious biases will not go away. So, if it is never going away, what is the point? The answer is we need to create a culture, where it is acceptable for people to call out bias when we see or hear it happening. My conscious bias is to believe we can get better at recognizing them and work individually and collectively to minimize their impact. We will grapple with this challenge in the coming chapters.

References

Kolodziej, A. 2015. "The Most Common Unconscious Biases Influencing Your Decisions." http://blog.allpsych.com/the-top-cognitive-biases-influencing-your-decisions/

Mahler, D.L. 2016. "Resting Bitch Face." www.louisemahler.com.au/project/resting-bitchy-face/

O'Neill, T. 2003. "Untouchable." *National Geographic Magazine*, June. http://ngm.nationalgeographic.com/ngm/0306/feature1/

CHAPTER 6

The Geometry of Inclusion

I always disliked algebra, and yet, for some inexplicable reason, I enjoy geometry. I could never find any useful way to explain that until now. When contemplating the inclusion journey, I realized that to more fully understand how to solve the inclusion challenge, we must understand the many angles of the diversity story.

When I think of the dynamics of diversity and inclusion, I think of the intersections and twists and turns involved in solving the Rubik Cube. I call this phenomenon the "geometry of inclusion" because it requires that we surface perspectives that barely make it onto our peripheral vision. Envision a Rubik Cube, and the vertical and horizontal lines defining the totality of the square. Additionally, there are subsections representing multiple horizontal and vertical blocks or lines. Within these angles, there is a veritable kaleidoscope of complexity hidden in plain sight.

The Vertical Axis

Most organizations view implementing a Diversity and Inclusion initiative as a vertical journey—starting from the top and working down through the organization. One of the key reasons for this is to ensure leaders are willing to commit time and budget and become active ambassadors and change agents to create an inclusive work environment. But, how do we make that change happen? Chief diversity officers and human resource leaders are charged with the responsibility to engage the hearts and minds of their leaders if they are to make progress. There is a pervasive and unspoken tension when you are charged with managing the diversity program for your organization. Looking at these questions faced by corporate change agents discloses the complexity and anxiety when launching a Diversity and Inclusion initiative.

1. What compelling evidence can we provide to prove there is a business case for diversity and inclusion?
2. How can we encourage our leaders to be active champions and ambassadors for this change initiative? How can we appeal to both their heads and hearts?
3. How can we avoid the pitfalls and obstacles that might cause our leaders to put the brakes on?
4. How do we manage resistance, particularly from "the frozen middle?"
5. What would encourage our leaders to keep forward momentum?
6. What do we need to do to win corporate awards for our efforts?

Why is this particular change so difficult? Surely it is just like rolling out a program on Lean Six Sigma or Total Customer Satisfaction? No, it is not that simple. Diversity and inclusion are seen as soft issues not necessarily directly related to the bottom line, and leaders and managers can often send mixed messages about their commitment. Just like parenting, people do not only listen to what leaders say, they watch what they do. If leaders roll their eyes when you tell them you need to attend an Employee Resource Group (ERG) meeting or they make it difficult for you to attend a diversity workshop, you likely will sense the incongruence between "corporate speak" and the reality of the mixed messages you are receiving. I recall a senior investment banker telling me she needed to drop her involvement with the company Diversity Council as she was advised by her manager it was side-tracking her career. If you hear leaders making comments or telling inappropriate jokes during an after-hours dinner meeting or in the bar, you are more likely to be influenced by that than the official party line espoused in meetings and at the podium.

Leaders need to be authentic and be aligned with the program, but we should also not expect our leaders to behave in a robotic uniform manner. Leaders are human too; they are not phenomenological exceptions, and there will be a variety of personalities, beliefs, and responses. There are leaders who get it and can express their support with sincerity and candor, leaders who pay lip service, leaders who remain politically correct, and leaders who engage in double talk. Nothing is as simple as it seems or as black and white as it might look. There is a multitude of complex feelings sitting around the inclusion table. I recently witnessed an African American male chief diversity officer change his story mid-sentence when he saw his White male CEO becoming uncomfortable about why race matters and why White privilege is a key part of that story.

Having said that, senior leaders typically are on board as they have seen the facts and been persuaded by the business case. The same cannot always be said for the next few layers of management as they may not be ready to own that this is a business imperative. This level of management is referred to as the "frozen middle" as actions (or non-actions) taken by them can block the success of any change management program, not just Diversity and Inclusion programs. Despite these challenges, the journey has to begin somewhere, and for most organizations, that "beginning" is to tackle gender inequities.

I recently read an article from Community Business in Hong Kong stating that the 2016 representation of women on the Hang Seng Index Boards has stagnated at a paltry 11.1 percent; zero percent growth from last year (www.communitybusiness.org/DOB/WOB/index.htm). Facts like these more than adequately establish a business imperative to justify why gender is selected as the first gateway.

I have also had numerous conversations with HR professionals and Diversity departments who say their organization wants to take a linear approach to the change process and focus initially and exclusively on gender. The following comments show a range of reasons:

We *only* want to focus on gender.

Our leaders are not ready to address other diversity issues.

Our leaders would not be comfortable discussing sexual orientation.

We are planning to hold race, culture, and sexual orientation, and so on on the back-burner until we reach our gender goals.

While it sounds logical to take a controlled and linear approach to diversity and inclusion and to pick just one group to be the focus of attention, it is not practical and cannot be contained. The minute you look at gender inequity, Pandora's box has been opened. The "butterfly effect" is in motion. Opportunity knocks as other groups raise their hands and ask "What about us? When can we come to the table?" Not to mention that women are not a homogenous group and will inevitably bring other diversity dimensions into the conversation. If, for instance, you are a lesbian woman of color with a physical disability, you might as well see the world through a different lens from a White heterosexual able-bodied woman.

There are also so many variables and complicating nuances to this story. For instance, while White women have been the gateway to a more inclusive environment, White women are also simultaneously viewed by other diverse groups not as the "gateway," but as the "gatekeepers" blocking the advancement of others, particularly men and women of color. The unspoken theory behind this belief is it is easier for men at the top of the organization to understand and work with White women.

Another hidden secret and little talked about phenomenon is while being the only woman or minority in a dominant group can be lonely, it can also give you the benefits and privileges of being unique and special. To the extent that when another woman or person of color joins the group, you may resent the intrusion rather than welcome the company. As the numbers increase, we move from being *the* individual spokesperson to being one of many and can get lost in the crowd; a situation we may not relish. A parallel dynamic is that senior women and People of Color can also become the de facto poster child for their diverse groups, and are expected to help explain the issues to everyone else. All eyes turn to them in meetings when diversity is discussed and they are expected to speak for their entire group. This often happens unconsciously as people turn to focus in their direction, sometimes causing people to think (or say out loud) "Why is everyone looking at me?" No matter how enthusiastically they accept that role and responsibility, they walk on eggshells needing to strike a delicate balance between being an ambassador and avoiding the pitfalls of being viewed as overenthusiastic or pushing the race or gender card.

Even when we agree to expand beyond gender to focus on categories, such as race and sexual orientation, we do not pay enough attention to the fact that there is work to be done to ensure each group is being inclusive of other groups. Hidden in the vertical axis is also the less obvious challenge of "*intersections*" between diverse groups. For instance, there is societal and historical tension between cultural groups, and yet, the term "People of Color" implies that they have a common purpose and common experience. In some ways that is true, but what is not always understood is there is not necessarily a common bond or compassion for the other group(s). I have been in conversations with members of ERG or Diversity Councils, where I was told by a Latino or Asian person they were embarrassed by African Americans always dominating the discussion or "playing the victim" and complaining about what life is like at work, and they want to disassociate from that. I have heard African Americans complain about Asians being viewed as "the model minority" and people complain about Latino groups speaking Spanish in front of them when the others only speak English or complaining that they can "pass" as White due to the color of their skin and get to choose which ethnic group they belong to on any given day. I have heard a gay member say another member of the Council is not gay enough. I have been told by a gay male that gay men do not always get along with lesbians, and yet, they are assumed to share

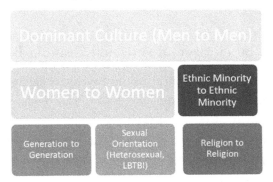

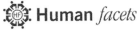

a common platform and expected to form one network. Also, there is an assumption when we talk about "White men" that we implicitly understand what we mean, and yet, it is fairly obvious that not all White men are alike. There is a lot of pressure on men to conform to a stereotype of what we think we mean by "being a man." Within that group, there are different age ranges, different religions, different sexual orientations, different personalities, and different degrees of alpha-maleness. I vividly recall a White male in a five-day workshop sharing with the group that while he cut a large and imposing figure and was often branded as an alpha-male, in fact, he loved music and art, and was afraid to tell his male colleagues at work. He had been bullied at school for not being interested in sports and learned over the years to fake more alpha-male behaviors he thought would keep him seen as part of the group. Similarly, White people need to be able to talk about what it means to be White. Did they grow up poor? Did they meet and interact with people of color or ethnic minorities growing up or did they see their first person of color when they went to University? When did they first realize "White" was being seen as a diverse group?

It is unrealistic to believe that we can ever fully resolve deeply rooted societal differences, and yet, if we are to make progress on inclusion, we cannot afford to disregard the elephants in the room. If the members of Diversity Councils and ERG do not stand in integrity with their own differences and recognize all of the diverse perspectives around the table; being willing to openly talk about individual and group perspectives and address the intersections represented and the societal baggage they may be carrying then, there is a strong chance that what they implement throughout the organization will miss the mark. So let's dig a little deeper.

The Horizontal Axis and Granularity

It is irrefutable that many organizations have been highly successful in moving the gauge on their D and I journey and have productively engaged their leadership as champions and advocates. They have focused on the vertical axis on categories, such as gender, race, culture, and sexual orientation. And yet, there is a need to explore the granularity of each of these horizontal groups. There are unexplored subtleties and differences within each group. They have rolled out effective Diversity programs and some have won awards and recognition for their efforts. Progress has been made, and yet, despite our best efforts, women and ethnic minorities are still underrepresented in the board room and at management levels. Not everyone is open to inclusion and not

everyone is on board. I spoke at a conference recently on inclusion and unconscious bias and when I shared some of my research to show the bias gaps that continue to exist for women, People of Color and other minority groups, a woman raised her hand and said, "Isn't that the way it is meant to be?," signaling that she actually believed that these groups were less capable, less competent, and it was OK to accept that as the status quo. I must admit to metaphorically raising my eyebrows while my inner voice said, "Oh my, she did not just say that?" When I asked her to clarify, she restated her belief that it was acceptable and predictable to see women and People of Color as less competent. Clearly, we still have work to do.

The fact remains the dominant culture(s) are still "dominant" and subcultures are still tapping on the glass ceiling or trying to untangle themselves from that sticky floor, or any other euphemism for inequity you care to mention. We have not yet arrived at a fully inclusive workplace. Women still earn less than men, and discrimination, both conscious and unconscious, continues to exist. I recently spoke at a conference where I was asked to be part of a series of breakfast meetings the following day. I was to share a breakout room with another speaker. When I arrived at the room and walked to my assigned table, the other facilitator (a White male) asked me what I was doing there, and in front of the 15+ people already gathered in the room told me he had the first hour and I could come back for the second hour. I tried to explain to him he was mistaken and that, in fact, there was only a one-hour slot and we were sharing it. He assertively proclaimed it would not work and he did not know what I was going to do, but I could not stay in the room. His behavior was not just rude and aggressive, but it exemplified all of the privilege and entitlement issues of male dominance and sexism. I told him as politely as I could that I would leave and given that my topic was "inclusion," I was going to spend some time reflecting on what exclusion felt like. The assembled group laughed and I left, but not without tucking another experience and another story into my inclusion notebook.

It would be so much simpler if we really believed in the unity of the human race. When we listen to Michael Jackson sing "We are the World," or watch Coca Cola and other companies run branding ads showing images of a world of difference portrayed as a celebration, you can almost hear a soul level sigh that says, "I wish it were so." It may be the way we *wish* it would be, but it is not the reality we see every day. As I write, I am watching daily reports of the migrant crisis in Europe and listening to the European Nations in conflict, juxtaposed with the individual heart-wrenching stories and pictures that tell a thousand tales. The illusion of "We are the World" does not seem to be where this particular story is heading, and with the enormity of that thought, I feel the need to retreat to the corporate arena, where the story is contained and manageable, and well-intentioned leaders are doing their best to figure out inclusion.

As I mentioned in the introduction, managers often tell me they treat everyone as individuals and don't really care about a person's diversity. Again I tell them, "But what if *they* care?" What if it is important to them that you understand their journey as a woman or a Person of Color or a member of the LGBTI community is different, and there is a myriad of examples where they experience being less valued? Most of us want to be treated as individuals *and* recognized as members of our various social identity groups. For instance, I want people to respect and understand my individuality and simultaneously recognize being Scottish, heterosexual, and a woman is an important part of my story and has shaped my experience of the world.

The paradox of inclusion is that, on one hand, we want to reduce it to all of us being the same—just individual human beings, but at the same time, we want to be seen as uniquely different. The crux of the matter comes when we consider some groups are different from others and some people within groups are different. Over the years, I have heard people say with some degree of frustration, "It is not *just* a Black-White issue," and while I believe that is often said as a defense against talking about racism, it is nevertheless accurate. Diversity is indeed much more complex; in fact, it is not just about the myriad of groups we could list, it is also about the myriad of variances within each group. Stay with me here. It is both/and, not either/or. It is not merely umbrella topics, such as race and gender, but all of the variances that come under each of these headings. There are as many diverse perspectives and characteristics within a diverse group as there are people.

It may seem like a straightforward delineation to ask people to speak about their social identity groups, but in my experience, it is not. There are people who are aware of their social identity and others who prefer to act as if it does not matter. Like everything else, we are discussing here, it is complex and often at times, replete with strong feelings and emotional baggage. Over the years of doing diversity and inclusion work, I have asked many people during workshops and experiential exercises to self-identify as members of a diverse group, for example, male, female, White, Black, Latino, Indian, Middle Eastern, heterosexual, LGBTI, Baby Boomer, and so on. Some people jump right in and do it enthusiastically and other people express resistance. Here are some examples of comments we have heard:

> I think of myself as an individual, not as a member of any group.
>
> I want to be treated as an individual.
>
> I don't want to be lumped in with the others in my group.
>
> I am not a racist just because I am White.
>
> Just because I am a man does not make me a sexist.
>
> I don't want to join the women's group for fear I will be identified as a feminist.
>
> I don't need all this attention being paid to my diversity; I am doing fine without it.

A fact often ignored in our top-down approach to inclusion is not everyone in the group agrees with the characteristics of the label, and we cannot safely make sweeping generalizations about a group. Just like giraffes all have unique patterns, it is no secret every human being has a unique DNA. We think of ourselves as individuals first and then we identify as members of social identity groups, such as gender, culture, and sexual orientation.

Individual versus Group

There is without question a dynamic tension between our individual and group identity membership(s). It is not either/or, it is both/and. We are *both* individuals *and* members of many groups, and whether we prefer to distance ourselves from them or not, other people notice them and label us accordingly. For example, you may not want to be thought of as a woman first; you may want to be seen as a competent individual, but my guess is the people interacting with you have already noticed you are a woman and are treating you accordingly. You may not want to acknowledge you are from a particular culture, but my guess is people are guessing anyway and trying to find a box to fit you in. The question that is wearily familiar to all immigrants is, "I meant where are you *really* from?"

If you take a moment to consider all the ways your group identity defines you, what insights would you gain? What characteristics do you share with other people from that group? What messages do you believe other groups have about your group—both positive and negative? In what ways, if any, do you work to identify with or distance yourself from your group(s)?

These questions can challenge your thinking, especially if you think of yourself as an individual first and foremost and believe you treat others as individuals. The "paradox of identity" is at the crux of the struggle with individuality. The answer is both/and. It is true that we are individuals, and it is also true we are members of multiple social identity groups. The comedy show "The Office" devoted an entire episode to pretending people did not notice someone was Black. In alignment with that thinking, there are people who believe so long as they are being fair and reasonable in their treatment of others that race and culture are "not an issue." In reality, other people do notice our group identity, and race and culture do matter. For the most part, we are not color-blind when it comes to race and culture, and we do see color. I recently heard about a man taken to the emergency room at 2.00 a.m., whose wife had an anxiety attack upon their arrival at the hospital when she discovered most of the staff was African American. She told a mutual friend, "They were all Black and it was awful." Apparently, both she and her husband were adequately taken care of and released within hours, but that fact got lost and superseded by her anxiety over her own racism and ability to notice and judge skin color rather than competence. Conversely, we may allow a person's color to unconsciously fade into the background of our relationship with them, as it is not the most figural part of our interaction with that person, but nevertheless, it exists and frames their experiences and color matters to them.

The first diversity workshops we facilitated in the mid-90s were experiential with lots of activities and story-telling. They were designed to enable people to share their stories and to educate participants on different perspectives. Over the years, I noticed consistently tensions increased as we discussed the different groups. There was a conscious and unconscious hierarchy of intensity in terms of which diverse groups it was "OK" to discuss. It was, for example, easy to discuss generational issues as everyone could relate to the topic, and it was not a threatening conversation; it was also noncontroversial to discuss people who were differently abled as we could all display compassion. But as we began to address issues of gender, the tension increased as men felt blamed and accused and some women became agitated and uncomfortable primarily because the *men* were uncomfortable. That discomfort paled in comparison to the arm folding, eye-rolling, and tension that mounted when we began to discuss race and culture. The current debate between "Black lives matter" and "All lives matter" typifies the tensions and misunderstandings we witnessed at that time and clearly not much has improved when it comes to understanding our differing frames of reference. When we then asked people to explore the topic of sexual orientation, the resistance in the room was off the charts and went from passive resistance to outright verbal objections, and on occasions, people would leave the room rather than participate in the discussion. The people who walked out or actively expressed their disapproval of the subject did not come from just one diverse group, they represented the spectrum of diverse groups and made me realize not only are we all individually different, but we have degrees of difference within each group. You cannot assume someone who is gay or lesbian is not homophobic, just as you cannot assume that a woman supports other women or all White men have the same views or someone who is an Indian was born in India. There is diversity within each group and degrees of difference that make a difference. Recognizing these differences should stop us in our tracks when we are tempted to make sweeping generalizations about the characteristics of any group.

You can probably guess by now what I am saying is when we only focus on the individual and we ignore another person's group identity and do not realize there is a back story, we are ignoring an important dimension of their diversity and inclusion journey. As we meet people, they move from being strangers to becoming individuals in our lives. There is value in being able to experience and learn from another person's story about their diverse group. There is value in seeing more in your peripheral vision and not limiting your story by your own experience or blind spots. Stories have a stickiness quality, and when we learn people's stories, they move closer to our inner circle and our vision of what is possible broadens.

Just like individuals, diverse groups also have stories to tell, and these stories are shared experiences across the group. For example, if I speak to a group about a woman offering a good idea and not being listened to, and then two minutes later, a man offers the same idea and he is told that it is an excellent suggestion, all of the women in the room laugh. Why are they laughing? Because that is a part of the shared experience of our group—as women we have either had that happen to us or seen that happen to other women. Comedians thrive on tapping into these shared group beliefs and stories and can guarantee that at least some of their audience will laugh when they recognize their group or group experiences being described.

Degrees of Difference

What has become increasingly clear to me is while we put the spotlight on core diversity categories, such as race, gender, and sexual orientation, and so on, there are multiple dynamics playing out within each of the diverse groups, which are often ignored. Embedded within the horizontal axis is the mostly unexplored granularity challenge of what I call "*degrees of difference.*"

These degrees of difference exist at every level across every group within the horizontal axis. The degrees of difference in the LGBTI community, for example, are based on judgments such as: Are you out of the closet? Are you not out? Are you too gay? What does "too gay" mean? Do gays and lesbians get along? People are judged, not just by heterosexuals, but by people in their own culture. What's the difference between being a lipstick lesbian and a butch lesbian? I vividly recall conducting a focus group in the UK for LGBTI employees, and a transgender woman was present. One of the gay men in the room pointed his finger at her and said, "You, yes you,—you are the reason that our heterosexual colleagues are afraid of us; you give our group a bad name." In the African American culture, the color line is a significant part of the story. The assumption being that the lighter the skin, the closer to White, and the closer to White, the more likelihood of acceptance and less discrimination.

When I was 10 years old I asked my mother where I was from. She looked puzzled by my question and reminded me I was from Scotland. I apparently became very indignant and proclaimed, "No, I am not. I am a citizen of the world." My mother was astounded by my response. I can honestly say to this day I have no idea where that came from, but looking back it was very prophetic. Today, I have accumulated over five million air miles and have traveled the world speaking about global inclusion and unconscious bias.

Of course, I *am* from Scotland and proud of it, but I am also aware of the myriad of other group identities I own. We all have *core* social identity groups, such as our race, culture, gender and sexual orientation; and then *primary* groups, including family, religious beliefs, education levels, geographical locations, and first language. We also have a third level of *tertiary* groups, such as our professional associations, workplace roles, and so on. My three levels include as core heterosexual Baby Boomer woman, Caucasian, European, Scottish, and an American citizen. As primary I am an extrovert, a PhD, an entrepreneur, a keynote speaker, a published author, and more. Within each of these groups, there are degrees of difference. For instance, not everyone who was born in Scotland shares the same perspective about being Scottish as I do and that is just for starters, as we have barely scratched the surface.

I have long believed we all have a hierarchy of biases tucked deep in our unconscious mind. There are groups we are comfortable with and groups we are uncomfortable with. We also have a hierarchy of bias *within* every group, and these hierarchies cause us to make judgments about people every day. They show up in our relationships and our decision-making processes, without us being consciously aware of them. When I moved to the United States as an immigrant from Scotland, I carried with me the assumption that because Americans speak English, it would be an easy transition. But it proved to be more challenging because Americans speak English differently. I find it very hard to give up the way I spell things. For me, even to this day, how I spelled things growing up in Scotland was the right way. I've given in now primarily because I lost the battle with my computer's spell check.

Another example of granularity and degrees of difference showed up when I was traveling in Asia a couple years ago. I didn't realize there's a hierarchy amongst expats. It's an informal hierarchy around how expats judge and include each other. It is based on such things as: How long have you been an expat? In how many countries have you been an expat? How well do you really know the local culture? How well have you integrated into the culture?

When I first discovered this phenomenon, I experienced a sense of hierarchy and superiority amongst expats, which seemed based on who had been there the longest. The innuendo in conversations was an implied "you don't get Asia and I do." It caught my attention as yet another degree of difference, and I began to ask people in conferences and workshops "How Western or Asian do you feel?" "Do you view yourself as 100 percent Asian and 0 percent Western or conversely, 100 percent Western and 0 percent Asian or anything in between?" When I first did that exercise, 2 to 3 years ago in Hong Kong, a White male from a major corporation stood up and declared to the group, he felt 100 percent Asian. No one in the meeting room believed he was 100 percent Asian. He didn't look 100 percent Asian. He didn't sound 100 percent Asian, and indeed he wasn't even 1 percent Asian. He was a White American male. But in his mind, he had lived in Asia for so long and had assimilated so profoundly into the local culture that he felt 100 percent Asian. To exemplify his point, he told the group his children ate with chopsticks.

We move seamlessly throughout the day in and out of our various group identities, playing whatever role works for us to survive and thrive. Without even realizing it, we leave parts of our personality in the parking lot in the morning as we walk to work and we pick them up again when we leave. Consider the group(s) core to your identity. Did you join them by choice? Or are they groups you are a member of because of family upbringing and part of your birth right? What messages do you carry, both conscious and unconscious as a result of your group membership(s)?

When you think about these groups? What are the many ways you individualize yourself in the group? For instance, you might make sure your family knows your uniqueness or ensure your team leader notices your contribution to the team. Are you the family jokester or do you know someone in the family who is? Or is there someone in your family or team who draws attention to themselves by being negative? Geert Hofstede's work on culture demonstrates there are individualistic cultures and collectivist cultures. It depends on the part of the world you were born, whether you value ensuring you are seen as an individual or prefer to remain part of the group. Australians have an expression, "Tall poppies will be cut down," when they sense people trying to rise above the efforts and achievements of the group. By contrast, in the United States, we have what I call the "John Wayne syndrome," where individualism is highly valued.

Social Identity and the Bell Curve

Every group has a bell curve with some people on each end and the majority in the middle. Some adopt the characteristics of the group 100 percent and others distance themselves from their group, preferring not to be referred to as a member and avoiding as much social interaction as possible, particularly at work. I have worked with senior leaders and male champions of change, who shared with me their surprise when they hear women tell them they do not want to be singled out as a woman and do not want to support any efforts to establish special programs to benefit women. Despite the fact, we celebrate International Women's Week and form ERGs for women, some women choose to distance themselves from other women in the workplace. I have had conversations over the years with senior women who tell me when they got promoted, they reached down and pulled the ladder up behind them. Their explanation being they had no energy to reach back and help other women as they needed to figure out how to thrive and survive alone in the C-suite. The same is true for other diverse groups. During an interview to discuss an individual's unconscious biases I have spoken, for example, with People of Color who admit disassociating from other People of Color, particularly from their own group. They explain to me they do not want to be seen spending time with their own group for fear of having their uniqueness lost in the milieu of being a minority.

The Tendency Toward Sweeping Assumptions

If we treat each other as individuals ignoring background, race, and culture and so on, we may believe we are being inclusive, but we are missing a huge part of who we are (and we know it). I was in a conversation the other day where some of my White women friends were discussing a book they read about slavery, and one of the women said her family had Black servants, and as a little girl, she played with the servants' children and never noticed the difference. When I said "but they probably did," everyone stopped talking for a few seconds and looked surprised. One of the benefits of dominance is privilege and that privilege allows us to not have to see that difference matters. We assume if it is OK with us, everyone else should also be OK with it. We assume if we don't see the difference, then the difference does not exist or does not make a difference.

And yet, difference does exist, and sometimes, when we first discover that difference matters, we feel guilty, clumsy, and confused, and perhaps, a little bit like Bambi first learning to walk. I spoke with an African American woman recently who told me now that her White colleagues have begun to understand the impact of White privilege, they are jumping uninvited to her defense even when she does not perceive any slight or mistreatment. While she recognizes their good intentions, she is troubled by the idea of them rescuing her from situations she herself does not see. They make sweeping assumptions she is the victim of racism and leap to her rescue. For the rescuer, it can be confusing. In their mind, if they say nothing, they remain complicit in allowing the racism to continue; if they say something, they run the risk of being seen as patronizing or rescuing people who do not see themselves as needing to be rescued. Where is the fine line and how do I learn to walk on it or straddle it?

Tools for Understanding the Geometry of Inclusion

Which tools might we need to more fully understand the geometry of inclusion? Should we create our own protractor? Which compass might be useful to set our direction and which ruler would work to measure our progress? If the journey to inclusion is indeterminably long, then how will we know when we arrive? The answers here are both simple and complex. Let's take another look at all the angles we are dealing with.

How well are we doing with the *vertical axis*? Are we creating a top-down initiative that is causing real change? Are we moving the gauge for women and other diverse groups? Are more diverse people showing up in the C-suite? Have we closed the pay inequity gap? Do we really have 100 percent buy in for inclusion? I think we know that the answer is "not yet."

Do we understand what we need to do to address the intersections? Do we acknowledge the fact that some of the diverse groups we are working with don't necessarily trust each other? Do we understand or even know they have their own truths, myths, folklore, and socially constructed stories about why that may be? Are we willing to lean in to all of that complexity, bring it to the surface, and agree to figure out what angle it would take for us to come together?

Then there is the *horizontal axis* and the granularity that appears when we scratch the surface on the degrees of difference within each group. When we look at each diverse group bell curve, we see people spaced along the continuum. Regardless of whether we look at race, gender, culture, sexual orientation, age, religion, or differently abled to name a few, there are members fully committed to their diversity at one end of the bell curve and people who prefer to avoid and deny their group membership at the other. There are people in the middle who know the challenges but don't care, and people in the middle who care but don't want to be involved. If we want to be sure to hear all voices and understand the issues more deeply, we are obliged to roll up our sleeves and dig a little deeper. We are challenged to listen harder, to lean in more, and to open our hearts and minds to hear perspectives we once dismissed or ignored as irrelevant. We may need an echo sounder or depth finder and a handful of courage sprinkled with staying power if we are to build trust. It would be the opposite of building a wall, a very large wall designed to keep people out. We would instead respectfully lean in and dismantle the walls. Our aim would be to figure out together what it would take to uncover the deeper issues keeping us from being an inclusive workplace, community, and society.

When we hone in on the degrees of difference, the simple solution is we need to start paying attention to the dynamics and variables within each diverse group. For example, it is not rocket science for us to accept that not all heterosexual Christian White American men are the same, and yet, we talk about that group as if they are. The more complex solution is we need to recognize that these internal group differences, which may seem insignificant, actually make a difference. We cannot take a broad brush approach and assume everyone in the group shares the same views and values. It is part of the reason we cannot get traction on inclusion. We make the assumption that all members are on board and they are not.

Just because we have a vision and mission statement that says, we value diversity is no guarantee we really do. We need to spot the ripples on the pond, to catch the glances across the table, the eyes rolling, the sardonic tone of voice, and the offline conversations and realize they mean something. We need to have the courage to generate conversations both within and across diverse groups in order to surface the tensions caused by our overarching assumption we already share a common goal. In order to answer these questions, we need to have the mettle to declare this a business imperative; to openly talk with each other, and become willing partners in the change process. Leaders need followers and followers need a purpose. Going it alone or in separate but unequal groups does not work and will not get us there. It just keeps us spinning our compass and using the wrong ruler to measure our success.

Reference

Hong Kong Hang Seng Index Boards. www.communitybusiness.org/DOB/WOB/index.htm

CHAPTER 7

Fighting the Force(s)

"Do or do not, there is no try," Yoda, *Star Wars*.

If you have ever tried to lose weight and failed or told yourself you will exercise more and given up a few weeks later, I am sure you can resonate with Yoda's well-known homily. "Try" is the weak link in the chain. The question it raises in the context of the immutable forces of inclusion is can we do it? Can we achieve mastery over them? Is it even possible and are we willing to do it, because there is no try?

It might be a stretch to suggest that if we are going to embark on this journey, we need to invoke the Jedi Knight within us to fight the power of these three immutable forces of inclusion, but at least we do need to harness our collective energies and commitment and become more consciously aware not only of their omnipresent power over us, but also of the compelling reasons for doing this.

The dynamics of dominance over subordinance, unconscious bias over conscious choices, and the complex nature of individuality and degrees of difference within groups are intertwined. If we were to tackle any one of these three forces separately, it would be formidable. When you look at the combined power of all three immutable forces, you are up against the tensile power of synergy and are fighting the odds. Is it impossible? No. Is it feasible? Yes, but only if we keep our eye on the inclusion prize.

The key here is to paint a clearer picture of the dynamics created by each of these forces, both separately and together. Taken individually, each of these three forces is a daunting roadblock to inclusion that reminds me of the well-known expression, "keep your friends close and your enemies closer." When you contemplate the impact of all three of them combined, you begin to realize the gargantuan magnitude of the task. Let's review each of them again with an eye on what we are facing and what we can do to mitigate their power and determine if there is an antidote that will weaken their ability to block inclusion.

It is an undeniable reality that there will always be dominant players and dominant forces. Dominance comes packaged with power, privilege, and a sense of entitlement, and as such is quite seductive when you have it. Are we stuck with a reality that the only thing we can anticipate changing is who is dominant—or can we at least tweak interactions between dominant and subcultural groups to improve relationships for the better?

When you consider the changing demographics in society and in the workplace, you can see changes happening before your eyes. Perhaps, all we have to do is let time take care of this, but I suspect this is not a good solution. Time will only create a tipping point where power and dominance will shift ownership, and inclusion will continue to be the loser. If we take the generational issues as an easy example, we see Baby Boomers are close to retirement; Generation X is currently in the career sweet-spot and the Millennials are carving their own path toward a new reality of entrepreneurship. And yet, it is a certain evolutionary fact that one day in the fullness of time, it will be Millennials who will be retiring. Today, White people are still the dominant culture in many First World countries, and yet, the demographics are changing, White families are having less children and ethnic minority groups are increasing in population size and power base. There is an interesting juxtaposition and irony, however, when we look at gender as women are demographically the larger group worldwide, and yet, men are dominant. There are more women in the world today; they make up the majority of most nations. More women than men attend colleges and universities, and yet, if I ask you if you can envision a day when women become the dominant culture you might find that hard to do. Why is that? Why are we not able to see a day when women are not only the majority in number, but the majority in the C-suite, the board room, politics, and world leadership? If sheer force of numbers is not the issue, then what is it? What stops us from envisioning a day in the foreseeable future when the gender power base will shift? The short answer is dominance and the privilege and power that go with it. It is very hard to give up power, particularly when you have history on your side.

And yet, giving up hope is not an option. In fact, I would argue there is no time in recent history when we need to figure out inclusion more than the present day because it is clear something is not working. There is a burning platform and compelling, time-sensitive reasons for us to tackle this. World demographics are changing and the power base of dominance is shifting. It is becoming more difficult to hire and retain top talent worldwide. I have a client where 60 percent of their manufacturing workforce is within five years of retirement. Baby Boomers are retiring and taking with them the knowledge and IP that drives many businesses.

One of the privileges of dominance is the ability to not have to listen to other perspectives or if you do hear them, to not hear them as credible. This is an opportunity gap. We can move a little closer to inclusion if members of the dominant cultures are willing and able to listen at a deeper level, open to understanding the individual stories they are hearing are systemic, and keep dominance in place. Think about conflict for a moment and consider the last fight you had with your significant other or child. Did it get resolved or does it just keep bringing up some of the unresolved history you have together? In order to resolve these deep-seated problems, you must slow down and listen at a much deeper level. Feeling dismissed and misunderstood is a much more significant problem than it first appears. I recently read results from a client's engagement survey where not being heard was on the top of the list of concerns that left them feeling excluded. They also listed not being treated with respect, feeling their stories were not understood and their ideas were not heard as credible. Feeling you have been heard is a large part of the equation and both parties need to feel heard and understood. That is much harder than it sounds, particularly as we live in an age of increasingly fractured attention.

It is important to create a safe space for conversations across differences where people can share their perspectives. Lip service, political correctness, and listening with one ear while interrupting to say "but that happens to me too" will not achieve that goal. Listening with an open mind and an open heart and being willing to make changes to create a more inclusive environment will take us in the right direction toward more collaboration. We may not agree with everything we hear, but we must be willing to see through the eyes of the beholder; to view the experience of the other without judgment and to allow others to feel fully heard and understood.

Once again, if I use the current U.S.-based situation of "Black lives matter" versus "All lives matter" as a template, we need to understand at a much deeper level why the "Black lives matter" campaign has such resonance for People of Color and particularly, African Americans in the United States, and until we do, we will never be able to reach agreement that "All lives matter." It is for them yet another example of why White people care less about their welfare as people and more about themselves. For instance, they would argue if Flint, Michigan, had been a predominantly White community, the decision that allowed the water supply to become contaminated would never have been allowed to happen. To improve understanding, we minimally must be able to identify with the concerns of a minority group and understand that inferior treatment is systemic and endemic and has significance for all of us rather than assuming it is an isolated incident. We are all one race and issues for the minority are de facto issues for the majority. We are all connected. We cannot write it off as their fault because it is due to poverty or lack of education. We cannot assume somehow they caused it or are to blame for it, or do not deserve better. We all need to lean in, listen, understand and then and only then can we can stand together.

Unconscious bias, as the second immutable force, is not going away either, but we can become more mindful of the many ways our biases stop us from making inclusive and respectful decisions. For instance, we pattern-recognize for competence and could challenge ourselves to identify that pattern and then change our mental models. A recent study published in the *Harvard Business Review* found non-White managers and female managers were rated as less effective when they hired a non-White or female job candidate instead of a White male candidate (Johnson and Hekman 2016). Conversely, it did not matter whether a White male manager selected another White male or a diverse candidate; there were no negative ramifications. Affinity bias was discouraged overall, but women and non-White candidates were judged more harshly for hiring in their own image. For people in subcultural groups, these experiences and reminders are like water dripping on a stone. They do not need to read the research to know it is happening, but when they do read the research, they send it flying across cyberspace and social media to all of their friends and colleagues as if to say "see I told you so; more evidence that I am not imagining this." Being willing to accept the fact that we are indeed treating other diverse groups differently both consciously and unconsciously and naming and calling out the biases will raise them to consciousness and begin to remove their power.

When we add to the equation the third immutable force of degrees of difference within each diverse group, we realize there is not universal alignment on what constitutes the needs or experiences of each diverse group. The inclusion work required here is for organizations to encourage conversations within and across diverse groups to surface these different perspectives, to more fully understand them and to work to close the gaps in understanding. Why do people disassociate from their own group? People within groups make choices, and not all of them are conscious. I am proud to be Scottish and love lots of things about Scotland and Scottish people, including golf, Scottish shortbread, and bagpipe music; conversely, contrary to popular opinion about the Scots, I do not drink tea or Scotch. When I first came to the United States, I did not join the Scottish Heritage Society as I wanted to fully experience what it meant to live in America and not just cloister myself within my own community. Degrees of difference make a difference, and we need to uncover these differences that are hidden in plain sight, allow people to be heard, and then hope to encourage them to abandon their desire to disassociate and join us on the inclusion journey.

Finding a Common Purpose

When you contemplate the vortex created by a combination of dominance, unconscious bias, and oblivion to degrees of difference, you see how easy it would be to be overwhelmed with the enormity and scope of the problem. How can we find a common purpose? It is certainly true; in the corporate world, we are not in the business of creating world peace, but we are in the business of enhancing the bottom line and improving productivity, and that can best be done when we fully utilize *all* of the diverse talents of our workforce. We have made the case that today that is not happening and many people feel under-valued, under-utilized, and not respected. We would also be naïve to believe what is happening around us is not impacting the energies people bring in to the office each day. Think about your own experience. What story are you telling yourself about inclusion today? It is more than just beauty that is in the eye of the beholder. When you think about barriers to you being more inclusive, what do you see? Do you understand your own shortcomings and your own passions/desires to be more fully inclusive or like the rest of us do you still have work to do? Are there unresolved biases and discomforts tucked away in the recesses of your mind that would hinder your progress and stop you from pinning that Eagle Scout badge of inclusion on your chest? Do you find your biases rushing to the surface as you watch the news at night and then tuck these thoughts away when you put your work face back on the next morning? What are your expectations and limitations, and from which frame of reference are you creating the story—a position of dominance and privilege or subordinance and oppression?

We need a reason to coalesce our energies around minimizing, if not mitigating these forces. Perhaps, we cannot make them go away, but can we work with them, and what are the possibilities of minimizing their collective impact? Would you entertain the possibility that the driving force for inclusion is the real and present danger of moving so far away from inclusion that it will take us centuries to gain back the ground we are losing? We need to come together within our workplaces and communities and remove the real and impending threat of a tipping point.

We each need to take ownership for how these three immutable forces play out in our lives, at work, and at home. We need to hold them up to the light, put them under a magnifying glass, and adjust our mirrors to honestly manage our blind spots. We should endeavor to become comfortable and adept at calling out behaviors that are obstacles and require adjustment in order to construct a more level and inclusive playing field. What can you do to lean in and more fully understand other people's stories and perspectives? Are you working to become consciously aware of your unconscious biases, and if so, are you working to remain mindful before making quick decisions? Are you aware of the nuances of degrees of difference and open to exploring this more deeply? Are you curious and courageous enough to learn, to ask, to listen, and to seek first to understand? Accepting the immutable nature of these issues and becoming more aware, taking ownership for the impact, and working to minimize or limit their negative effects is mission critical in a world that is becoming increasingly unsafe and less inclusive by the day. May be people think we are doing OK on this journey to inclusion, but because I am looking at the world around me through the filter of inclusion, I see a different story. Just look at the news every day and you will see our desire to be inclusive bumping up against the changing global demographics, the graying of the workforce, divided communities, contentious politics, terrorism, hate-mongering, and more. We are at a point where we are fighting very negative forces that may be here for 10 or even 20 years. We are heading in the wrong direction as a global community. You could not be blamed for throwing up your hands and saying, "What is the point? Why bother to work on inclusion?" Rather than viewing diversity and inclusion as a soft issue, as not related to the bottom line and seeing the immutable forces as inevitable, the corporate world is in a unique position to influence and educate many people who are not only employees but members of society. The kryptonite and the burning platform that will overcome these forces and drive us toward inclusion is that this is necessary for the continued survival of civilized society as we know it. If the majority of us, whether dominant or subculture members, took the mission of inclusion seriously, perhaps, we could head off some of these challenges or at least slow them down.

Inclusion is a workplace issue, but I contend this workplace issue has taken on a bigger role in recent years and has significant ramifications for societal problems. The business world can make a difference if we choose to. We need to join forces and fight for inclusion as anything short of that will precipitate a downward spiral, which will not serve us. If we invoke the Jedi Knight within us and look the obstacles to inclusion straight in the eyes, we could make a wider difference than just in the workplace. In doing so, we should mindfully take the advice of Yoda when he said to Luke Skywalker, "A Jedi uses the force for knowledge and defense, never for attack." May the force of inclusion be with you. The alternative is not an option.

Reference

Johnson, S.K., and D.R. Hekman. 2016. "Women and Minorities Are Penalized for Promoting Diversity." *Harvard Business Review.* https://hbr.org/2016/03/women-and-minorities-are-penalized-for-promoting-diversity#

CHAPTER 8

The Permeable Forces
of Inclusion

Oh what a tangled web we weave when first we practice to deceive.
—Sir Walter Scott

Have you ever been less than honest during a conversation about diversity or while speaking to someone from a different gender or culture, either to protect yourself or to ensure you did not hurt another person's feelings? Are you aware of being politically correct on occasions because what you were thinking and what you felt the need to say was not in alignment? If so, you are not alone. The tendency toward "little white lies" (why are they called "white" lies anyway?) and political correctness is unfortunately built into a system of coping mechanisms designed to help us handle the impact of the three immutable forces we discussed in the previous chapter. These coping mechanisms are directly related to the permeable forces that are essentially leading us away from inclusion.

Learned Behaviors and Coping Mechanisms

There are *four* permeable forces, and just like the three immutable forces, they are inseparably linked. They grew organically out of a need to cope with the presence of the immutable forces (Figure 8.1).

They are so insidious and pervasive that they keep us spinning our wheels around the inclusion axis. They are affinity bias, assimilation bias, political correctness, and stereotype threat. Permeable forces, by their nature, are porous, pervious, and absorbent. The inclusion permeable forces are almost guaranteed to leave us thinking we will never arrive at inclusion, but the good news is since they are permeable, we can get through them. In the case of our search for inclusion, they distinguish

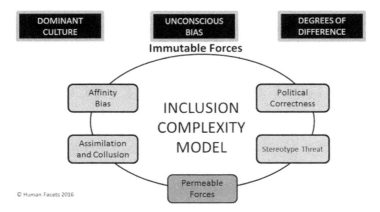

Figure 8.1 Human Facets: Inclusion complexity model (2016)

themselves from the immutable forces discussed earlier because they are learned behaviors and coping mechanisms, which help us deal with the existence of the immutable forces. These forces have come to be because of the need to *maintain* dominance and paradoxically, the need to *survive* dominance.

In a nutshell, *affinity bias* causes us to hire in our own image and surround ourselves with people who make us comfortable. *Assimilation bias* causes us to adjust our style to ensure we fit in with the dominant culture(s) and make them comfortable. *Political correctness* creates situations where we think one thing and say another, and *stereotype threat* is the negative impact on members of subcultures, caused by the messages they receive from the dominant culture(s).

Cause and Effect—Maintain and Survive

My client was proud of the fact she had a diverse team. She was new to the company and had inherited most of her team members. She told me three of her team members were from other countries and spoke several languages. She brought me in to help with team building as she felt people were holding back and she could sense tensions in the group. I interviewed all of the team members and observed some team meetings. People told me about their discomfort with other team members and a common theme was discomfort with the leadership style of my client, and their new boss. She was described as a micro-manager, paying too much attention to detail and too task-oriented. She had an assertive personality with a tendency to interrupt people at meetings when the conversation was not heading where she wanted. People adjusted what they were saying midstream when they sensed from her body language she was displeased. They also told me she had favorites, and if you were not one of them, you did not get listened to. When I observed the team meetings, I began to notice that team members who spoke English as a second language did not speak up very much and were not invited to offer their opinions by the boss or any of their colleagues. Most of her eye contact went to the one White male and the White women in the team, and it did seem, prima facie she was favoring them when allocating key assignments. During a one-on-one conversation with my client, she shared with me being an Asian woman, originally from Vietnam, and now living in the United States, she experienced discrimination. She felt today she had to assert herself in order to not be seen as one of those quiet Asians everyone talked about and took advantage of. She tried not to associate with other Asians as she felt she would then be labeled a minority and not noticed by leadership. When I asked her about her Asian and Indian team members who seemed reluctant to speak up at meetings, she first said she had not noticed and then after a few minutes of reflection added "Well *I* had to figure out how to be more assertive and they should learn to do the same." She went on to reluctantly admit that during a recent performance evaluation for one of these team members he asked her why she did not seem interested in his opinions and ideas at meetings and she had denied that was happening; she told him he just needed to be more assertive to ensure his voice was heard over the crowd.

Wrapped up in this story are examples of the permeable forces, in particular affinity bias, assimilation bias, and political correctness. My client, as an Asian woman, showed a strong affinity for the White women and one White male as she wanted to be accepted by them. She unconsciously paid less attention to other Asian team members as she did not want to associate too much with them and risk being seen by dominant culture members as just another Person of Color or showing favoritism to her own group. Her team members were displaying assimilation bias in their efforts to quietly fit in with what she appeared to want. What she said she wanted was for them to speak up and find their voices, but the didactic manner in which she conducted her team meetings left little room for group discussion and openness. The bottom line for my client was she wanted to succeed, not just survive, and to do so, she learned coping mechanisms *that gave* her a much better chance of holding it together. Aligning with the dominant culture members, minimizing her involvement with the subcultures, being frustrated at them for not copying her style, and asserting her voice at meetings were all unconsciously held strategies driven by previous discrimination and how she experienced an environment of dominance. There is a domino effect and that is multiplied by everyone in the room who is experiencing their own version of this.

Blind Alleys and the Rubik's Cube

In our efforts to work on inclusion and assist subcultures, we have occasionally spent time and money going up blind alleys. In an effort to help women and other diverse groups to "fit in," it is even possible some of the practices and solutions we have previously implemented sent the wrong message and created more of a problem than they solved. For instance, sending women to Assertiveness Training does not solve the pay gap or create a more equal and level playing field; it merely serves to reinforce the idea that somehow women's style is not a good fit and they must be helped to be more assertive. Ironically, when the pendulum swings and they become more assertive, other less-flattering labels are used to describe them. Sending subculturally diverse groups to efficacy training is like moving one piece of the Rubik's Cube and expecting that will solve the puzzle; when in reality, it is the entire Rubik's Cube that needs to be solved. We are all in this together, albeit pushing or pulling on the same piece of rope and sometimes in opposite directions.

Can We Form New Habits?

We often tiptoe around the vagaries of difference and you may well argue this is all part of being professional and civilized. I would not disagree and am not advocating we throw caution to the wind. However, I do want to surface here that in order to cope with the impact of immutable forces we have learned behaviors that do not necessarily serve us well and most certainly are barriers to inclusion. These behaviors are the result of the "permeable forces." The bad news is they exist because of our very efforts to cope with the tensile power of the inclusion immutable forces, but the good news is we could unlearn them, or at least, we can catch ourselves in the act and make a more inclusive decision. It is possible by raising these issues to consciousness that over time and with practice, we can expand our thinking and exchange these engrained habits and coping mechanisms for new, more productive skills. Taking a closer look at these forces individually will help us do that.

CHAPTER 9

Familiarity Does Not Breed Contempt

When it comes to diversity and inclusion, the old adage "familiarity breeds contempt" is not strictly true. I would contend familiarity, for the most part, does *not* breed contempt but it breeds comfort and complacency.

We may become complacent with our similarities, but in reality, we are creatures of habit and do not easily or naturally embrace differences. We prefer to find people who share our values and beliefs and align with our ways of being, rather than trying to stretch ourselves to include differences. We like things to be for the most part predictable with just a little bit of excitement thrown in for good measure. The brain loves to habituate, and we are creatures of habit. We want to know our routines will not be rattled and we can count on things to be where we left them, or be comforted by our meals being on the table at the time we expected, and the Wi-Fi at our home to work without problems. Affinity bias nicely captures the essence of habit and familiarity as it describes the propensity to surround ourselves with people like us whose values make us comfortable. It is also one of the major barriers to inclusion of difference.

Over the years, I have watched an interesting phenomenon unfold. As much as we want to believe we are willing to be inclusive, when we throw too much diversity into the mix we can be left feeling uncomfortable, resistant, and perhaps, even somewhat threatened. When there are a few diverse people, it makes things interesting. When there are a lot of different groups coexisting, it is viewed as multiculturalism, but when we add too many people from any one diverse group (other than the dominant culture), it can shut down enthusiasm for inclusion. It does not matter whether they are moving into the neighborhood or joining a team. If your golf, tennis, or bowling club was predominantly one group and has begun to "change" in the recent years, I am going to guess there are disgruntled conversations happening among the original members. Why do I know? Because I have heard the comments and been in these conversations. People do not like change. Why is that? Perhaps, it is the difference between graciously sharing space on occasions and feeling your space is being permanently invaded, and along with it, values and customs are being changed around you.

If I made a hierarchical list of unconscious biases and their impact on retention, *affinity bias* or mini-me syndrome would be a top contender. Affinity bias is often defined as a form of interview bias resulting in the interviewer hiring and promoting others similar to themselves. However, I argue it has much more wide-ranging ramifications. Affinity bias goes much deeper than our hiring practices. It shows up in all kinds of subtle ways, impacting the day-to-day decisions we make.

A few weeks ago, I called a customer service hotline seeking assistance with a recent purchase. The young woman on the phone spoke quickly in a very flat monotone, which suggested to me she was reading a script. No matter what question I asked her, she repeated the same script back to me. My blood pressure was rising and my patience was wearing thin. It seemed likely from her accent that she was not a native English speaker. Eventually, I asked to be put through to a supervisor, and a few minutes later, I heard a familiar American voice saying "Hello, this is Mary, how can I help you." Ah, I had been transferred to a "mini-me." Affinity is easier. My breathing began to normalize, I started to feel more relaxed, and I began my story again feeling confident I would now be understood.

After the call, I found myself wondering how often I notice I am breathing easier around people who are like me. I suggest this almost unconscious physiological reaction is impacting trust, and inevitably affecting the quality of relationships and the decisions we might make. At the epicenter of being inclusive is the need to stretch ourselves to allow more people of difference into our inner circle and to learn to breathe more easily around differences. But the question is how we do that? There is a way, but it all starts with awareness.

We are much more at ease with people who align with our values and our customs and much less relaxed with people who behave in ways we find a little "strange" or who challenge our thinking or disrupt our "normal" ways of doing things. Intellectually, we may believe we like to surround ourselves with people who think differently, but if we are being honest with ourselves, we can only take so much of that before our tolerance level is overstretched. Irritation at difference can show up in simple ways. I have heard employees complain about other groups hanging out together in the cafeteria, while not being cognizant they also are "hanging out together." We meet and marry people for their uniqueness and then spend the rest of the relationship trying to change them. We would much prefer to have people agree with us and conform to our style and way of doing things. If we are being honest with ourselves, it is irritating to constantly have our views challenged.

You could make a pretty convincing case that preferring to be with someone who makes you comfortable is not only part of the human condition, but also a part of the biodiversity ecosystem. We don't normally think of a lion deciding to hang out with leopards or a hippo deciding it would be cool to abandon the group and go hang with elephants; and if they did, we would probably be watching a Disney movie and thinking it was cute. Even domestic pets like cats and dogs, while they may peacefully coexist in the same household, left to their own devices are drawn to sniffing around with their own species. When we see a picture of a turtle sitting on the back of an alligator, we may smile or raise our eyebrows in wonder, but in reality, we don't really think that is a good idea. So why would we expect humans to be different?

In truth, we all have a natural propensity to not just be around people we can relate to, but also generally we prefer people who agree with us. Is that such a bad thing? Is affinity bias such an entrenched part of human behavior that we cannot hope to change it? And, if it means being biased toward "people who make me comfortable" or "people who are like me," then surely somewhere tucked in the recesses of our minds is the shadow side "people who make me uncomfortable" and "people who are not like me"? Ironically, we are curious, interested, and intrigued with difference so long as it does not impose itself on us for too long. For example, we can go on a vacation to another country for a couple of weeks and find the local culture and customs unique, charming, and quaint. However, if the same people and customs moved into our neighborhood, we might quickly stop considering the experience charming and quaint.

Embracing differences is easier when we are on a two-week vacation to another country and have willingly paid for that diverse experience; it is different when we meet people of difference in the cafeteria every day or turn up our nose when we smell their food in the microwave at work. Is it just that we are resistant to change or is it anxiety because we fear our customs and ways of being are being eroded or subsumed by other ways of being?

Unraveling the Complexity of Affinity Bias

To widen our inner circle and include others who are not like us, we must take a few risks, open our hearts and minds, change our mindset, and be willing to expand our thinking.

So, the real issue behind asking people to move away from affinity bias is that we are encouraging people to widen their inner circle, expand their in-group, and include others not like themselves, in the hope they will learn to value their diversity and behave inclusively. We may even begin to appreciate each other and become more comfortable with difference.

In addition to being caught on the treadmill of affinity bias, we can also fall into the "illusion of inclusion" trap when we say we value diversity but insist on assimilation behaviors. We do this by having a diverse team or organization and then creating a culture where everyone must conform to the dominant culture norms, de facto holding back their best selves.

It is important to hire employees who fit into the culture, but are there unintentional negative consequences to having too tight a definition of what a "good fit" looks like? We obviously want people who will fit into the team and with the values and ideas of the organization, but may be without realizing it, we also fall victim to affinity bias and inadvertently shut down or not embrace anyone who might have a different point of view. It is possible to surround ourselves with people who are diverse and then not allow their differences to surface. How can we be sure people feel motivated to bring their best selves to work?

Is being a "good fit" a good thing? Are we limiting our options and not being open to more diverse candidates, diverse personalities, and diverse ways of thinking, if we have a mental model that suggests what a "good fit" looks like? We say we want diverse candidates and then we quickly acculturate them to fit into the work environment and become part of the status quo. Employers look for candidates who are not only professionally skilled, but to whom they can relate. As organizations seek to find and retain diverse candidates, they are increasingly turning the spotlight on our human tendency toward affinity bias.

To limit the chances of affinity bias in the hiring process, many corporations are ensuring they have a diverse recruitment panel to add different perspectives to the discussion. Some companies remove names from resumes during the first round of the recruitment process to limit initial bias; however, I suggest that only puts a Band-Aid on the situation; after all, eventually the hiring manager will figure it out. Simultaneously, water-cooler discussions of reverse discrimination, political correctness, and questions about whether we have gone too far with the diversity and inclusion agenda continue. "Are we lowering our standards for the sake of diversity?" is a frequently heard question in the corridors of privilege.

When we talk about affinity bias in the context of the workplace, the subtext of that conversation tends to imply that we are primarily asking the dominant culture, namely White men, to recognize the need for more diversity. While that is accurate, it is only one piece of the story. We all have a predisposition toward affinity bias, regardless of our race, culture, gender, or other diversity group memberships. Affinity bias is not the exclusive right of the dominant culture, we are *all* guilty of it, and yet, there is an incongruence lurking in the shadows. Paradoxically, it is still much more difficult for people from subcultures to hire or promote people in their own image. I recently interviewed an Indian male manager of a Research and Development lab for a major U.S.-based Fortune 100 Company. He told me when he was hiring, he was always careful not to hire people from his own culture as he did not want to be blamed for being biased. He observed that perhaps he was not being fair to his own people. He noticed his colleagues from the dominant culture did not seem to have to worry about that to the same extent. Additionally, he said he walked the lab daily and made a point of saying good morning to everyone, with the exception of people from his own culture, whom he ignored for fear of being accused of favoritism.

Who can we blame for this proliferation of dominant culture-driven affinity bias in the workplace? Is it really today's senior White men? I see them rolling their eyes in quiet desperation as they anticipate being blamed yet again. We all play our part in keeping this situation in place. The distinguishing differences between White men in leadership and all other groups of employees are power and status. They have the power to not only continue to proliferate the hiring of other White men, but to also suggest to women and other diverse groups it would not be the best career decision for them to hire another person who looks like them. The HBR research mentioned earlier found that all other diverse groups are judged harshly for hiring in their own image, but there were no negative ramifications for White men hiring other White men (Johnson and Hekman 2016). When members of the dominant culture hire or promote or even hang out with people who look like them, it is part of the fabric of the organization; when people of color or women hire or promote other women or people of color or go to lunch with only women or people of color they are noticed, it is, in fact, part of the burden of difference.

If you are surrounded by people who look like you, have the same values, love to do the same things, and make you comfortable, then you are not pushing any boundaries, which means you probably have too much affinity bias happening. The goal is to challenge yourself to include people in your team who are different from you, different cultural backgrounds, different personalities, and different in their thinking styles.

While moving beyond affinity bias to ensure we have more women and people of color moving up through the ranks may seem straightforward and just a numbers game, it is not. I admit paying attention to the numbers will help—we should not take our eye off that demographic ball as it is a tangible way to measure progress; however, affinity bias is an unconscious bias and operates at so many subtle and insidious ways that it is way too easy to keep it alive and functioning.

I live in a small neighborhood with some White, Black, and Latino neighbors and notice that left to our normal disposition the people who cut our respective lawns all match our culture. My African American neighbors hire African Americans, my Latino neighbors hire Latinos, and I hire white Europeans—funny how that works. It is natural to lean toward people who make us comfortable, people who speak our language.

Are we bad people, are we being racist, are we consciously excluding others? Do we just naturally resonate with people who get us? I cannot speak for my neighbors, but I am much more comfortable speaking to people who "get me" and to whom I can easily relate, and there is nothing inherently wrong with that. Now, I do have tradesmen (they are men) who are from other cultures, but they are typically sent by the phone company or the cable company, and so on. My point about the lawn care is when we had the choice we all hired people from our own culture. If you unpack that a little further you could argue there was more than affinity bias going on, perhaps, the subcultural groups were giving work to people from their own culture to be supportive, and perhaps, I and my other Caucasian neighbors were acting out of our privilege and not even realizing there was another choice—and perhaps, it was a little bit of all of that. You see, affinity bias is not the exclusive right of the dominant culture; we all practice it. Why we need to focus on it at a corporate level is because of the glass ceilings, glass walls, sticky floors, and ongoing inequities. It is not the individual homeowner making their own decision about lawn care needs that matters as much; it is the endemic and systemic nature of institutionalized oppression, which still exists in the workplace that causes us to need to pay attention to the bigger pictures and the ongoing inequities. There is and always will be a dynamic tension between our individual preferences and rights to choose and the line that we cross when discrimination, bias, and institutionalized inequities become the norm.

Breaking Open the Affinity Box

A few years ago, one of my corporate clients staged an evening event for the recruitment companies they used to attract and hire diverse employees. They had a panel of high-profile leaders who each spoke passionately about the business case for attracting and hiring diverse talent and urged the recruiters to find them diverse candidates. The evening was going well and on schedule until we reached the Questions and Answers part, when one of the recruiters raised his hand and said, "I have been listening to your case for action and it is all very well, but when we present 'diverse' candidates to your hiring managers, we are told either directly or in code that they want a White male. We get paid on deliverables, and do you really think we are going to look for diverse candidates when we know your managers don't want to hire them?" The room erupted in a sea of nodding heads and acquiescent muttering, and you could feel the air come out of the balloon as the panel members realized the significance of the comment. It is not enough for the leaders to be saying the right thing; we also need to convince the "frozen middle" of the benefits of inclusion. We need to approach inclusion like we would approach a Lean Six Sigma program. I heard someone recently saying, if you accept 99.9 percent accuracy rate, then that would be like accepting two unsafe landings a day at Chicago O'Hare (or your local airport) and the post office losing 15,000 pieces of mail a day.

How does affinity bias show up at work? Let's start with the obvious areas, namely the hiring and promotion process. Affinity bias shows up at three levels: the obvious and measurable level where you can see the results of your bias in the hiring and retention demographics and the less obvious where you are networking with people whom you like and the more subtle level where you may not be conscious of your actions, but other people notice.

Obvious and measurable:

- Who would you prefer to hire?
- Who do you see being hired?
- Who do you see as the best fit for the job?
- Who do you see getting the promotions?

Less obvious:

- Who do you choose to socialize with?
- Who do you trust with that important assignment?
- Who do you not trust?
- Who do you share information with?

More subtle:

- Who do you make eye contact with at meetings?
- Who do you instinctively shake hands with?

- Whose voice do you hear as credible?
- Are you mindful of your unconscious bias and blind spots?

Take a moment to consider how affinity bias shows up for you in each of these categories. Who do you automatically include? Who is merely on your peripheral vision and who gets excluded? Who wishes they were in your group that you choose not to see?

In order to breathe more easily with people who are different, I need to get to know them and become comfortable with them. Affinity bias is not going to go away, so, what we need to do is feel affinity for more people of difference. We might need to move outside of our comfort curve to achieve that, but perhaps, it is a good place to start by paying attention to our reactions and then learning to breathe more easily when we are interacting across differences. Research demonstrates that heterogeneous groups produce more creative results than homogenous groups, so, why is affinity bias so compelling? In part, it is because it requires more work and more time for a diverse group to come together. Affinity with others is easier.

I recently spent time with some friends from Trinidad, and they introduced me to a man from the UK, as I was the only other person in the group from the UK. We had an immediate affinity, and I found him looking across and making eye contact whenever he felt there was a point in the conversation where he would expect me to be culturally aligned. We did not discuss the topic, we never agreed to agree, we never analyzed those moments, and yet, we just knew we understood each other's point of view. We were all discussing food and he mentioned the "Fish and Chippy" and looked over at me for affirmation; we both laughed and I added a comment about eating out of newspaper and putting malt vinegar on our chips and we laughed again. Later in the conversation, he commented on the Scots eating haggis, prompting me to tell the tale of the three-legged creature in Scotland called haggis. Cultural affinity runs deep and we make a lot of assumptions about each other both inside the group and across groups. What was noticeable to me, and perhaps to him also, is how comfortable I felt in the warm glow of those moments of connection and inside jokes. When surrounded by our own culture, we take it for granted; when we move away from our culture, these interactions become precious gifts to treasure in a sea of difference. When I lived in Scotland, I did not react to another Scot in the elevator or hearing another Scottish accent, but take me out of Scotland and you would think I discovered a long-lost cousin when I hear someone speaking with a Scottish accent. I become excited and immediately ask them where they are from in Scotland and we become instant friends, if only for a few moments.

On another occasion, I specifically requested my limo service from my home to the airport and not send me an SUV (Sports Utility Vehicle), as I prefer a sedan. But when the car pulled up in my driveway, it was an SUV. So, I walked outside with the intent of letting the driver know I would be a few minutes and that I was upset they had sent an SUV. As the driver got out of the car, my attitude and approach changed mid-stream and I put the brakes on my stream of consciousness as I realized he was an older British gentleman who reminded me of my father. Affinity bias, "mini-me" syndrome, racism, unconscious bias, it's all mixed up in my reactions to people, and I remain convinced when thinking about diversity and being inclusive that if bias lives in my body, it lives in yours. We need to be able to move our unconscious biases from the back of our neck to the edge of our shoulder; where we can at least see them in our peripheral vision and then, we might have a fighting chance of catching them and making mid-course corrections.

If you accept my premise that affinity bias, or other forms of unconscious biases, are part of the human condition and are not going to go away, what can be done to ensure we all behave in an inclusive manner and value diversity? We are not going to rid ourselves of affinity bias, so, we need to feel affinity for people different from ourselves. We might need to move outside of our comfort zone to achieve that, but perhaps, a good start is paying attention to our reactions and then learning to breathe more easily when interacting across differences.

Here are some questions to consider when thinking about affinity bias in your own life. Where does your affinity bias show up? Who do you spend time with? Who are your 10 best friends at home and at work? Have you noticed your physiological reactions to difference? What could you do to build more intuitive trust across differences?

Stretching the Box on Affinity

Prima facie, this looks easy to fix as we just need to hire and promote people of difference. However, it is not that simple. Even if you have diverse people in your team that does not mean you are behaving inclusively toward them. It is also possible for people to be part of your affinity groups, and yet, their personality or appearance might leave you feeling you do not have any particular affinity toward them. The challenge is not to get rid of our propensity for affinity; quite the opposite.

We must increase the size of the box we operate in: to stretch our boundaries and allow more people of difference into our center of influence, to work to be more comfortable with different styles and encourage different styles and different voices.

Is your team diverse? If not, make a conscious effort to bring in more diversity. What questions can you use to monitor your tendency toward affinity bias? How could you encourage more diverse voices? Who are you more comfortable assigning important projects and asking for ideas and inputs? If you are more comfortable giving important projects to people who look like you and/or mirror your style and value you, then take stock of what you can do to widen the circle of people you trust. Pay attention to how you conduct meetings. Do you invite all voices to be heard or are there people you do not listen to or find credible? If so, what is it about their diversity that shuts you down? Who are you ignoring and why? It is easy to be with people who agree with us; it is more courageous and creative to be willing to be challenged by difference. Are you willing to expand the box and let other people in?

Reference

Johnson, S.K., and D.R. Hekman. 2016. "Women and Minorities Are Penalized for Promoting Diversity." *Harvard Business Review.* https://hbr.org/2016/03/women-and-minorities-are-penalized-for-promoting-diversity#

CHAPTER 10

We Cannot All Be Idiosyncratic

You could have heard a pin drop in the room when he spoke.

I was facilitating an Unconscious Bias and Inclusion workshop in Australia, and we were discussing assimilation (the need to fit in) when he raised his hand and said:

I was born in China and I came to Australia when I was five years old. When I was 18, I moved from Perth to Sydney to attend University. Today, when I look in the mirror I do not see someone who is Asian, I see an Anglo-Australian. I think of myself as an Anglo Australian.

Wide-eyed stares of disbelief met the speaker's words. No one else in the room saw an Anglo-Australian. But he said it so clearly and with such compelling intensity that no one dared argue. He spoke to me during the tea break, his face wrought with consternation as he said, "The problem is, Helen, I've lost my culture." In order to fit into the dominant culture, he had abandoned his own culture. Worse than that, he'd stopped seeing his authentic self. His face told the story. It made me grieve for his sense of loss as I could almost hear him wondering how he could recapture what he had given up.

The pressure to belong and be accepted by the mainstream is intense and underestimated. The challenge of differences at work today is not only who we exclude, but how much we work to maintain the status quo. How much pressure do we subliminally put on people who are not members of dominant groups to figure out how to fit in and be accepted? How much pressure do they put on themselves? Feeling the need to anglicize your name is one indicator; working to lose your ethnic accent or disassociating from people in your own group is another. For women, talking about sports when really not interested in sports is another clue, or using bad language to be seen as one of the boys. It does not work, but does not stop us from trying. White men not interested in complying with the alpha-male image also have to assimilate and may pretend to be interested in conversations about sports, drinking, and other topics when in reality, their values are not aligned.

In the business world, most people work hard to fit in and conform to the expected norms of organizational culture. There are exceptions. If you are an important revenue generator for the company, then you may be implicitly granted extra bandwidth to be idiosyncratically different. In reality, being different may be trending, but only if you are iconic. Lady Gaga is idiosyncratic and iconic, and people pay a lot of money for her concerts and music, but having your differences accepted by the mainstream is more challenging if you are not a superstar or sports icon. For most people, compliance and conformance is the norm. It is true some employees work to stand out and be noticed by their leaders, but that is mostly contained within the bounds of conformity and being a team player. Conformance, however, can be the enemy of innovation, and maintaining the status quo is guaranteed to stifle creativity and risk extinction. Taxi drivers did not see Uber coming; hotels did not envision competition from Airbnb; Barnes & Noble did not see the emergence of Amazon; and Kodak could never picture the day smartphones would significantly undermine their raison d'etre. What are we missing when we do not see the value of allowing differences and not assimilation to flourish?

Compliance Is the Norm

Assimilation (and its inseparable twin of collusion) is probably the most complicated of the four permeable forces. It takes two to tango and both parties are complicit because neither the dominant or subculture members are consciously aware that assimilation and collusion are happening. The need for conformity created a mini-monster we call assimilation. Assimilation is what people do to fit in with the intent of ensuring the dominant culture is comfortable, and collusion happens as both groups consciously or unconsciously select not to notice it happening. People shrink the size of their personal circle of influence and operate at less than their potential for fear of being seen as not a good fit. Comments made during the hiring, promotion, or performance evaluation process that suggests the person is not compliant with the expected cultural norms would raise the question about their "fit" for the organization and can also be code for "I am not comfortable with their difference." Women and other diverse groups are highly attuned to these clues and subtle messages; hence, the reason for learning to assimilate.

I am not advocating we adopt a laissez-faire approach where anything goes, but am suggesting we need to become aware of this hidden force and productivity drain and create more safe space for difference. If we want people to bring their best selves to work and not just their minimal self, we need to expand the boundaries of the box. Oftentimes, people express their creativity and talents outside of work; they are musicians, craftsmen, artists, poets, writers or actors, but if we could capture that creativity and bring it back to the workplace the benefits would be exponential.

In order to put our work faces on, we all leave pieces of ourselves in the parking lot each morning, but some diverse groups have to leave more of themselves than others. Subculture members do not necessarily realize how much they adjust their style to fit in. They become so seamlessly skilled at doing it they no longer notice. It has become a "natural" part of their modus operandi. There are a myriad of ways in which the dynamics of assimilation show up, and just like affinity bias, we move seamlessly in and out of it on a daily basis without even realizing we are doing it. A gay colleague shared with me recently when he worked in the corporate world, he used to laugh at comments heterosexual men made about women as he wanted so badly to fit in and not to raise any suspicion. Within different ethnic groups, people are sometimes referred to as coconuts or bananas—brown on the outside and white on the inside or yellow on the outside and white on the inside, and women are assigned the "B" word when perceived to be trying too hard to act like a man.

Given all these labels and the amount of anxious energy to try to fit in, why do people do it? We learn in a multitude of unconscious and conscious ways to adjust our style to keep ourselves safe, to be accepted, to be included. Children intuitively and quickly learn to sense when parents are angry; you knew before they spoke, just from the look on their face or the pallor of their skin that they were angry and you became adept at quickly adjusting your style to try and avoid their displeasure.

Assimilation behaviors are an energy drain for the individual and the organization. In large part, they mean we are holding back and it takes energy to hold back. What is the organization losing when you make yourself "smaller" and withhold parts of your authentic self? Why can we not just find our voice and be ourselves? The pressure to fit in and be accepted is more intense than we realize, and messages abound within the culture, both organizational and societal, as to what it takes to be inside the normative bell curve. This pressure is driven by the underlying impact of the immutable forces, particularly the concept of dominance.

When people do not feel safe to bring their best selves to work they withhold ideas and constructive feedback for fear of rejection and stop offering their creative and innovative ideas because they no longer believe they will be listened to. This can happen to anyone and is not exclusive to subculture members as White males also assimilate to be accepted. We send overt and covert messages to employees about what they need to do to fit in. People intuitively sense what they need to adjust and minimize their style accordingly. But, what do we lose when we have so much conformity? We lose commitment, productivity, engagement, loyalty, creativity, and innovation. The 2015 Gallup poll shows that 51 percent of employees are disengaged at work and 18 percent are actively disengaged (Adkins 2015). Are you fully engaged? If not, why not? How much do you personally work to ensure you are not excluded? To put it another way, how much do you adjust your style to ensure you fit in and conform to the status quo? Have you been in a meeting where you did not speak up and express your true feelings or watched someone else do that, despite knowing what they said before the meeting was not congruent with what they were now saying? People hold back; people expend their energy adjusting their style. If we could gain 10 percent Return on Investment (ROI) to the bottom line by making it safer to offer new ideas from a different perspective, then surely we should ask ourselves where the line is between iconic and trending and how we can expand the box to let more people in.

But, a large part of the problem is members of dominant cultures are not aware when others adjust their style to fit in because it is not on their radar screen. They are only likely to notice when someone makes them even slightly uncomfortable or when they occasionally or perhaps, rarely find themselves as minority. For instance, being the only White person at an Indian wedding, the only straight person in a gay bar, or the only man at a woman's conference.

For dominant culture members, the work of spotting assimilation and minimizing its impact is hard. What do you have to know or do to spot when people are adjusting their style to be accepted by you? How can you let go off your need for people to conform to your cultural norms and make space for people to bring more of that difference to the table? How do you expand your concept of what a "good fit" looks like to make room for difference? Not easily, that's for sure. Between the propensity for affinity bias and the omnipresent accommodations of assimilation wrapped up with our unconscious collusion, it is difficult to spot and even harder to unravel. We might have to go through a level of discomfort to create a new normal. A little scary, right? Again, this calls for awareness, ownership, honest reflection, and courageous conversations across differences. We might have to initiate conversations across difference to discover what people feel compelled to do to keep you comfortable. And then, we would have to step up and commit to expanding our operational box in order to create a safer space for people to offer more of their best selves at work.

It is also important to acknowledge that the need to fit into society, organizations, and groups is not all bad. In fact, it is necessary in order to avoid anarchy and chaos; we cannot have teamwork without collaboration and compromise, and not all performance feedback is invalid. As you can see, the assimilation onion has many layers. Three of the ways the assimilation dance manifests in the workplace is through performance feedback, distancing from our own group(s), and collusion with the person doing the assimilating. Let's peel back these three layers and take a deeper look.

Assimilation Onion: Performance Feedback

Have you ever been told you need to tone it down? Can you please use your inside voice, be less aggressive, demonstrate more presence, have more gravitas, don't be so pushy, be more assertive, don't be too shy, speak up more, and so on. It is not always easy to digest performance feedback, but the raison d'etre is pretty straightforward and self-explanatory. Or is it?

All of us must adjust our style to fit in at work. Somewhere between home and work, you put on your "work face." You don't think about it, you just do it. It happens unconsciously and seamlessly, you move from being "Me," the person you are when you are moving about your personal life with friends and family to "Me," the professional. When we first join an organization, we quickly learn to read the norms of the organizational culture. If we are going to survive and thrive, there are many ways in which we seamlessly adjust our style to fit in, but as one of my client colleagues said, "I don't want to have to turn myself into a pretzel every day in order to be accepted."

Throughout our careers, we get our share of performance feedback direct and indirect, formal and informal, solicited and unsolicited. Our brain is hard-wired to ignore the positives and focus on the "development opportunities" that tell us we need to change something about who we are to fit in. Developmental feedback often makes us feel defensive, insecure, and dejected, and we usually must work hard to rationalize the story by convincing ourselves it really is for our own good. When we receive positive feedback, we might talk about it for a little while; we will probably tell our loved ones that evening at dinner and call a few friends, but if we hear negative feedback, we talk about it for the longest time and tend not to forget it. There is feedback and then there is *feedback* and the way we internalize it is filtered through lots of layers of our experience, including our race, culture, gender, sexual orientation, and so on.

From all of the stories I heard throughout the years, there is a pattern surrounding feedback, which is more than the sum of its parts. There is helpful and developmental feedback and then there is feedback that appears to have a stickiness quality and hints of confirmation bias. For example, my research results show men are more likely to be described as exhibiting leadership qualities, being assertive, and career-driven, and women are more likely to be described as lacking gravitas or being too pushy.

Here are some questions I ponder when I think about feedback through the lens of diversity and inclusion. Is it possible some of the feedback is a product of unconscious bias? Is it possible well-intentioned purveyors of feedback are not consciously aware that their preference for affinity bias influences their judgment about differences? Is it possible the mental models and stereotypes we carry about a group influence our thinking in the direction of confirmation bias (i.e., looking to confirm what I already believe)? Is it possible that when you receive this kind of feedback, you view it through the lens of your gender, culture, or race, and not just as a development opportunity? Is it possible the feedback you just received to "tone it down" is the same feedback many of your social identity group colleagues receive? For example, if you are told, as a woman, you lack presence and gravitas … is that valid, or an unconscious gender bias?

When we think about professional development and performance feedback, we are typically addressing things people need to do to "fit in" to the corporate culture. If you think metaphorically of your corporate culture as a large square box and then ask yourself what does being a "good fit" look like, then what must someone need to do to be considered a good fit, to be allowed to play inside the box? How does the meritocracy play out? Is there really a level playing field in your workplace or do you see bias and affinity issues? How do you know when someone is not a good fit? What criteria are you applying?

We coach people until they fit into the box, or conversely, put them on notice and ask them to leave. What if we expanded the size of the box to allow more diversity of thought, style, personality, creativity, and innovation? What if we sent the message we value different ways of thinking and want to hear different voices—do you think that would allow more people to bring their best selves to work?

Can you think of examples when you felt like your ideas were overlooked? Can you think of a time when you might have overlooked someone's ideas based on your personal affinity biases? There is a price we pay when people do not feel safe to speak up; there is a huge difference between compliance and commitment. If by being more inclusive we could gain more leverage on commitment and productivity, do you think our corporate leaders would be interested? There is a bottom-line business impact from diversity and inclusion.

When we cover up our best selves, there is an energetic price we pay for it. As the mantle we carry all day disappears and we fade back into being "the real me," most of us find we're exhausted and feeling negative because we haven't been our best or authentic selves from 9 to 5.

Assimilation Onion: Distancing

Separating ourselves from our own social identity group(s) is another piece of the puzzle. I had a conversation recently with a client who shared she never feels comfortable talking about her own ethnic group and sometimes feels ashamed to admit her country of origin because of its poverty and not wanting to be associated with that. She would like to be able to identify her country of origin, but feels she cannot, in case it causes other people to think less of her. I know senior women who try not to be associated with the women's group as they do not want their senior male colleagues to think of them as a feminist. They are afraid if they are seen to be advocating for women's issues or labeled as a feminist it will hurt their reputation and career. A recent article in HBR highlights the point that women and People of Color are being penalized for their association with diversity (Johnson and Hekman 2016). I was working with a client recently when one of the leaders of the women's Employee Resource Group told me her boss made it abundantly clear her involvement with the company Diversity programs and initiatives was putting her career and job at risk. This kind of pressure makes it very difficult for subcultural group members to feel comfortable, bringing their best self to work and maintains the need for assimilation behaviors.

This kind of distancing behavior happens all the time in subtle and not so subtle ways. Can you relate to this? Do you have attitudes and beliefs that live inside your head and cause you to negatively judge members of your own group or distance yourself from them?

We are all on this see-saw or Ferris wheel together. If we assume only subcultural groups should be the focal point of our inclusion efforts, we will be missing a critical piece of the picture. If we succeed in achieving more inclusion for all of the subcultural groups while leaving out White men, we will have created a tipping point, and 10 to 15 years from now, there will be a whole new group of Diversity consultants running workshops to include White men. White men also assimilate and cover up parts of themselves to play the role expected of them. Not every man is an alpha-male, not every man likes sports, and not every man feels the need to demean women while socializing in male only groups; however, I know many men who go along to be seen as "one of the boys." Just a few weeks ago, I had a conversation with a man who told me that he knows nothing about sports and loves classical music, but he is not always comfortable admitting that. He learned to ask questions about "the game" in order to sound like he is involved, but actually he could not care less.

Assimilation Onion: Collusion

Have you ever been speaking and adjusted what you were about to say mid-sentence because you sensed the listener was not going to be receptive? When we sense that we are in precarious situations, we become adept at scanning our environment and reading the nuances and subtle shifts in facial expressions, body language, and tone of voice. We listen for certain phrases that raise red flags and then imperceptibly shift our style and adjust what we are saying to accommodate the other person and keep ourselves politically safe. We do not necessarily agree with the listener's reactions or responses, but recognize the warning signals and know if we want to live to fight another day we need to smooth over the situation. I have watched clients change their story as they talked to their executives about diversity and realized they were not being heard or sensed the atmosphere in the conference room was not welcoming; I have done it myself, both at home and work, when I realized my listener was not receptive to hearing the message; we all do it, but the question is—where does it really leave you as the speaker? Do you dig deep to find more courage to speak up or do you quietly adopt a learned behavior of assimilation to survive and fit in?

Collusion in the context of assimilation is the process of adjusting our style to ensure we keep ourselves politically safe and we keep members of the dominant culture comfortable. Over the years, I witnessed many instances where people have accommodated others in the conversation while all the time knowing that they held a different view, but felt the person was not ready to hear it.

The late Dr. Roosevelt Thomas Jr. used to talk about the fact that if you build a house suitable for an elephant, a giraffe will have a hard time fitting in. I offer an added dimension. If a giraffe had to turn itself into a pretzel to fit into the elephant's house, I think we would notice, but if the giraffe were shrinking just a little bit every time we interacted with it, we might not spot it happening. The question is how much energy, creativity, and passion do we lose when we have a miniature giraffe? Could we be more productive, more innovative, and more creative if we made the box we play in bigger and allowed more space for difference?

A few years ago, I attended a one-day event where we discussed the differences in perception across cultural groups; it was an honest and very authentic conversation that surfaced some negative impressions of each group. When an African American male shared his story of discrimination, one of the senior White men in the group expressed skepticism that the incident was racially motivated, suggesting these things happen for him too. During dinner, while I was sitting next to him, one of his African American male employees jokingly said, "So, you hate my people, but you still choose to work with me?" They both laughed and continued with their dinner, almost as if it was a male bonding moment. It takes two to tango, and I wondered if either of them realized the powerful draw of assimilation in that moment. Would you?

References

Adkins, A. 2015. "Majority of U.S. Employee Not Engaged Despite Gains in 2014." *Employee Engagement.* www.gallup.com/poll/181289/majority-employees-not-engaged-despite-gains-2014.aspx

Johnson, S.K., and D.R. Hekman. 2016. "Women and Minorities Are Penalized for Promoting Diversity." *Harvard Business Review.* https://hbr.org/2016/03/women-and-minorities-are-penalized-for-promoting-diversity#

CHAPTER 11

The Wolf in Inclusive Clothing

If you are a smoker, you know what society thinks of you. You see the disapproval in nonsmoker's eyes. You live daily with the inconvenience of huddling in corners where you are "allowed" to smoke. If you are overweight, you are keenly aware of society's judgments about obesity. You see people looking at your food choices as they nibble on their designer salads, and you hear unkind and derogatory comments about the other "fat" people around them. Of course, they don't mean *you*, but you cannot help but take on that label, adding more heaviness to your already obese burden. I have a male friend who thinks it is funny to tell women, who are overweight that the simple solution to losing weight is to rub olive oil on your elbows and push yourself away from the table. He usually regales you with this comment as he is consuming his share of a large piece of chocolate cake. If you are a Person of Color you know what society says about you. You have heard all the stereotypes, and chances are high you have felt the pain of those stereotypes in a myriad of ways. If you are gay or lesbian, you know what society thinks about your group? You have heard the comments; you have seen the repulsed faces of your colleagues, who do not realize you are gay, while they tell jokes or speak disparagingly of other gay people, expecting you to agree with their views and laugh along with them. If you are a White male, you also know what society thinks about you. You have heard the comments about dominance, privilege, and entitlement, as you struggle to understand how growing up poor could possibly have put you in a privileged category.

We know full well that people have a negative view of us based on certain habits, emotional or mental challenges, physical disabilities, stereotypes, and predispositions. What we do not see quite as clearly is the impact of these judgments on the individuals who are the focus of this negativity. We do not see clearly that some of the behaviors "those" people demonstrate are, in fact, a direct result of having the negative judgment reinforced in the fabric of the society around them. They pick it up like a mind virus and then wear it like an invisible mantle.

There is nothing rational about stereotype threat and internalized oppression. But, it is all too real. It is a conscious and unconscious admission and acceptance you and members of your group rank lower in the societal hierarchy. A sense of being inferior and somehow "less than" becomes deeply embedded in the psyche. It says to the overweight person, they are less important than thin people; to the gay person, he is not the norm; to the Person of Color White is better; to women, that men are superior. In all of these messages, there is an uneven power dynamic. The vicious circle continues in perpetuity. We hear the negative messages. We learn to hate ourselves. We then direct that disdain toward ourselves and each other. We do the very things the stereotype tells us we do. We make bad food choices to console ourselves from being overweight and feeling judged. We are often more critical of our own group than we would be of others. We may distance ourselves from members of our own group for fear of being "associated with them." Being gay or lesbian, for example, does not necessarily mean you have compassion for other LGBTI people.

I recall speaking with a senior military officer who had become a strong advocate for gender equality. He told me he was very surprised that it was the women officers who were complaining to him about his efforts to help women. He said they were adamant they had achieved success without help and did not want to see other women get "special treatment." He was confused by this seemingly contradictory message. And yet, it is all wrapped up in the morass caused by internalized oppression.

We cannot fix a problem until we see it. We want members of the dominant culture to "get it" and step up to partner with us and fix the problem. But the problem is made more complicated for dominant culture members when the very people they are trying to help tell them they don't want or need help. Or you witness people "not helping themselves" when you think they should be able to. Or, as in the case of the women telling their military officer they did not want other women getting special treatment, they seem to turn on their own group and you are left confused and wondering "well, if they don't like each other why should I care." In this scenario, no one wins and it can end in a stalemate. And so, the vicious circle is kept alive.

An African American male consulting colleague once told me, in Black families when a baby is born, the first thing they do is check behind the ears to see if the baby will have light skin and hope they will have "good (non-kinky) hair." Internalized oppression shows up in many ways. It also shows up in the use of derogatory epithets groups use to refer to themselves. For instance, calling people "Sambo" or "Uncle Tom" to refer to others who try to act White or have too many White friends or using the "N" word as a term of affection toward each other are all signs of internalized oppression.

Stereotypes show up in an insidious manner. People do not say to your face, "listen, I am about to stereotype you as lazy, or overweight, or less intelligent." It is not that simple. Negative messages come in all kinds of packaging. The messages you are considered less valuable than another group can be microscopic, but constant in nature. Something as small as not making eye contact, not shaking hands, not touching a person's skin as you give them something, not trusting they can do the job, to larger biases, such as not giving that person a job opportunity, or a bank loan, or not being willing to visit them in their neighborhood while expecting them to come to yours. I was recently speaking to a tradesman at my home who has worked for me before. When I first met him he was very overweight and seemed lethargic, but his team did excellent work and so, I continued to work with him. When I met him again recently, he had lost 25 lbs. and was looking much better. He was more energized and enthused about himself and his work, and I found myself responding to him more positively. I later reflected that being overweight myself had not stopped me from noticing and unconsciously judging him and then being more friendly to him when he was thinner. It is subtle, insidious, and painful. Sometimes, it is not until we "change for the better" that we realize how badly we have been treated and have been treating ourselves. The problem with that premise is not everyone who experiences prejudice and is the victim of internalized oppression can or should change. If you are a gay male, you cannot choose to not be gay; if you are Black, you cannot choose to not be Black. Although I vividly recall listening to a young African American woman tell a group of our workshop participants, when she was a young girl she tried to scrape her skin with a knife to see if she could get rid of the Black and become White. About 15 years ago, I was working with an African American female colleague. We had and still have a very good relationship, and once when I was working in her city, she invited me to stay overnight at her house. I thought nothing of it and we had a really fun time together. After the trip, I sent her flowers to thank her and she told me later her husband said I was a different kind of White person because I was willing to come and visit them. I am sure there are lots of stories like this, and I am not a phenomenological exception, but on that day, her comments hit home as I never really thought about the fact most of the time that White people did not want to go into her neighborhood. There are so many things we do not see about each other's stories and experiences, and one of the things we do not see is the impact of the constant negativity. It is not the unbearable lightness of being; it is the unbearable burden of knowing.

On a personal level, I live with this unbearable burden of knowing and not just because of my gender. I have been overweight for quite a few years and have an auto-immune thyroid disorder, which does not help me to lose weight. It is a source of great consternation to me and I think about it daily. A few years ago while at a consulting event with some of my colleagues, we were sitting outside having lunch. The hotel had provided a buffet, including a table with mini desserts. I walked over to take a look at them and was trying to decide if they were worth the calories when one of my male colleagues took me by the elbow and led me away from the table, saying, "Here, let me help you with your decision, you don't need that." I am sure he was well-intentioned, but the pain of his judgment did nothing for my self-esteem. The irony of internalized oppression is this albeit well-meaning intervention can have the opposite effect. To ease the pain, I wanted to find something "nice" to eat. The vicious circle internalized oppression sets up is that you are irrationally driven to sabotage yourself. The illogical, almost knee-jerk reaction of doing exactly what "they" expect of you takes over your brain cells. I am aware as I write this of the fear welling inside of being judged as not having enough will power. Perhaps, I will go and find something to eat while I think about this.

Red Flag: You Don't Know It When You See It

It is not so easy to spot or pin down evidence of the existence and impact of stereotype threat or internalized oppression. Stereotype threat is a self-confirming belief you may be evaluated based on a negative stereotype of your group. Internalized oppression is how you internalize and act out those negative messages. The belief about that evaluation then causes you to underperform due to anxiety and anticipation. It is pernicious and maleficent, and most often, operating outside the consciousness of the individual. Stereotype threat can cause individuals to underachieve and can arise when they find themselves in situations where you sense societally enforced negative judgment. Something as simple as filling out the demographics on a form and naming your race, culture, age and/or gender, just prior to taking a test or going to an interview might unconsciously reinforce a stereotype that reminds you that your group is not expected to do well on this type of interview or test. Research also convincingly demonstrates that reminding people of negative expectations for their group causes them to underperform. For instance, reminding a woman that women are not expected to be good at math could result in poor math performance or reminding a Baby Boomer they are not expected to be technically savvy or social media competent could result in them failing a web-based test. When stereotype threat is removed, people perform better.

I would be the first to admit that just mentioning the words "stereotype threat" sounds very academic, and it is certainly true there is an impressive body of academic research, which has been conducted to demonstrate the power of this particular phenomenon; in fact, in full transparency, my PhD dissertation focused on internalized oppression and stereotype threat. However, I also want to be sure that in addition to the academic rigor behind the research, we remember to humanize the story and reinforce the fact that the impact of stereotype threat can have a profoundly disempowering effect on people's lives. What may look like a simple case of poor self-esteem can actually be driven by internalized oppression and stereotype threat—where powerful societal messages convince that you are not competent or talented in certain areas of your life.

Internalized oppression is the implicit acceptance of the societally based prejudices against them and that acceptance takes on a life of its own.

I know people like listening to my Scottish accent, and as I have mentioned, I also know being overweight is judged negatively. I receive lots of positive comments about my accent and thankfully, I get very few negative comments about my weight. And yet, I am more focused on the negative stories in my head concerning my weight. We have a propensity toward the negative. If the nightly news was 55 minutes of good news and five minutes of bad news, we would only tune in for the last five minutes. So perhaps, not surprisingly, while the weight of *evidence* is in favor of the affirming messages about my accent, the *burden of anxiety* I feel is focused on the negative messages about my weight (which are not voiced, but internalized).

I don't focus too much of my energy on the positive impact of my accent and often forget about it until someone says "I love to listen to you speak," which is a regular occurrence. Conversely, the negative judgments about being overweight weigh heavily on my mind at all times; although I have very little tangible proof people are making that judgment, I have a deep and painful knowing. I hate being overweight in part because I know society looks disparagingly at overweight people and not just because I know, it would be better to lose weight.

Negative labels and judgments make us put defenses in place to cope and stuff the pain. This results in low self-esteem and self-sabotaging behaviors. Stereotype threat is like a drone hovering over us that guarantees negative self-fulfilling prophecies. If the societal story is negative, this, in turn, causes us to think less of ourselves, downplay our importance, damage and contort our self-esteem, and sabotage ourselves and each other.

One of the pernicious problems with stereotype threat is it keeps you constantly anxious. If you know your diverse group is stereotyped for being late and you are late for work, you will feel the burden of the group on your shoulders. If you know your group is seen as not being as competent as another group and you make a mistake, you will carry the additional burden of that message. The anxiety you feel may also make you perform worse than you would if you were not worrying so much. A female consulting colleague of mine told me the story about working with a female client a few years ago who gave her many mixed messages. She would tell her how brilliant she was and then tell her she did not think she was bright enough to understand what she was saying. The steady stream of like versus dislike messages alternated to keep my colleague off-balance, and if there was a chance of making even a simple mistake in the client's presence, she said she somehow managed to do it, accompanied by a sinking feeling she had just confirmed the client's negative impression of her. She also did brilliant work and managed to steady the ship. But, it took additional work and was not enjoyable or a good use of energy.

When she later analyzed the situation, she realized the praise was as much out of context as the negative messages, which were anxiety-provoking. My colleague was aware of the need to protect herself from misrepresentation and of the huge amount of anxiety this behavior was producing. Sometimes, positive comments can inflict the burden of the group on the other when the suggestion is "you are not like the others in your group; you are better than them." If, for example, you carry a stereotype that Latin people are always late and then a Latin colleague or employee arrives early, you might express overly enthusiastic delight that they are early. That message is not picked up as a compliment as the receiver knows what you are really saying is they are an exception to their group norm.

It would seem simple to write this off as just one individual relationship challenge, but the problem is, it quickly taps in to the insecurities we carry about being a member of whatever group we identify with. Just as water finds its own level, tension finds the weakest link. Once we are infected by the memes or mind viruses of internalized oppression, it will not matter what the "perpetrator" intended, the message goes to the open wound and the vicious circle continues.

Examples of stereotype threat messages abound and include commonly held urban myths, such as Asians are not expected to be good drivers, men are not expected to raise the children or to be house-husbands, overweight people are not expected to have will power, women are not expected to understand car mechanics. There is a considerable amount of research to demonstrate the toxic and pernicious impact of stereotype threat, including the classic Clark Doll Test when Black children were asked questions about Black and White dolls, such as "Pick up the good doll" and "Pick up the bad doll." Most of the children preferred the White doll and assigned positive traits, such as "good" or "pretty" to the White doll and "bad" and "ugly" to the Black doll (Clark 2016). The study has been repeated in recent years with similar results (Edney 2006). Other well-documented examples include women perform worse in math tests when they think the test will produce gender differences (Spencer, Steele, and Quinn 1999). White men perform worse on math tests when they think they are competing against Asians (Aronson et al. 1999). White male golfers perform better when they are competing against African American male golfers and are told the measure of success is the ability to think their way around the golf course; they perform more poorly when they are told the measure is physical ability (Steele 2010). Female chess players perform worse than male chess players when they are aware they are playing against a male opponent. When they are (falsely) led to believe they are playing against another woman, they perform just as well as the male players (Maass, D'Ettole, and Cadinu 2008). When orchestras suspected gender bias was playing a part in their hiring decisions, they decided to conduct blind studies. They placed a shield between the judges and the candidates, and advised the female musicians not to wear heels or perfume. The result of the study was the number of women members of major orchestras today has risen from 5 percent to 25 percent (Goldin and Rouse 2000).

Among all of the obvious ways in which stereotype threat negatively impacts individuals and the self-fulfilling prophecies that flow from it, there also lurks the shadow of the confirmatory judgments being made by other people. "See, I told you 'they' (insert any diverse group where you have a bias against their driving) were not good drivers, and this just confirms it." Or, "I knew we should not have hired a woman for that job; they just cannot handle the pressure." What we do not realize is we may be picking up the wrong signals about why the person failed to meet the criteria. We may be making judgments confirming our negative stereotype, when in fact, the individual is being impacted by the very same messages that our dominant group imposed on them. Again, we are pushing and pulling on the same rope, and not realizing we are all in this together.

A few years ago, I interviewed an employee originally from Hong Kong who was at that time living in Australia. I noticed in her unconscious bias assessment results, the group she was most uncomfortable with was Asians. She told me she was not surprised since she spent her entire career trying to distance herself from other Asians. She felt if she was seen associating with them she would be stereotyped and not taken seriously by White people and in particular, by the people in leadership. When she reflected on the results of her assessment and mulled over her experiences, she came to the conclusion she needed to change that. She said she had been thinking about returning to Hong Kong, but resisted doing so because of her irrational fear of blending in with her own culture. I have no idea if she made the move, but based on our conversation that day, I am persuaded she was keen to reconnect with her people, but overcoming her internalized oppression was an incredible challenge.

There is an inextricable connection between the beliefs and attitudes perpetrated about a diverse group, the messages picked up by that group, and the fact that they turn these messages on themselves and each other. They hear the messages around them and unknowingly drink the Kool-Aid. They subconsciously become convinced they are inferior and may then act according to the stereotype. And then, in a spectacular act of circular logic, the rest of us get to confirm that we were right to believe that they are not capable after all.

What Can We Do About Stereotype Threat?

We are all in this together. It is not as simple as dominant groups perpetrating the messages and subcultural groups internalizing them, acting out on and then being judged in a confirmatory manner for those actions. It is further complicated by the fact that every one of us has multiple social identity groups within us, including our race, gender, sexual orientation, religion, personality traits, height, weight, age, and so on. This can cause us to not easily identify which set of negative messages we are reacting to. Am I down on myself because I am a woman? Am I critical of myself because I am overweight? Do I distance myself from other White women because they are White or because they are women or because they are from another country, or because I just don't like them as an individual? It could be a little of everything, or something entirely different, but how will you ever know? So long as you are infected with the memes of internalized oppression, it becomes a common denominator, and you are going to have to keep revisiting that open wound and the insecurities it manifests.

Is there any good news in this story? Is it possible to overcome internalized oppression? Yes, but as with everything else we have discussed, it starts with awareness. We all need to become aware of the impact of internalized oppression and its close cousin, stereotype threat. It has been clearly shown negative reinforcement begets negative behavior, creating loss of self-esteem and loss of motivation and productivity. It has equally been shown reinforcing positive behaviors can produce positive results, so perhaps it could be as simple as all of us remembering to be positive toward each other. Oh well, you cannot blame a girl for dreaming.

In "Whistling Vivaldi," Claude Steele talks about the young Black male student who noticed White people crossed the street when they saw him coming, and when he learned to whistle classical music, they no longer crossed the street. They even smiled at him as they passed (Steele 2010). If he was whistling a rap song, I will speculate the White people would still cross the street. The young man knew that whistling was not enough; he knew he had to learn to whistle something that was favorably recognized by members of the dominant culture. The existence of stereotype threat is so powerful that it can totally change your behavior. It becomes a coping mechanism and the individual creates contingencies to cope with the contingencies they face just because they are a member of a diverse group. It is not visible to the naked eye, but people make subtle adjustments to their behavior all of the time to make sure they keep themselves in the acceptable zone when interacting with members of the dominant culture.

In my case, I have fought the inner gremlins and internalized damage from all of the negative messages about women for many years; it has caused me to intermittently hate myself, fear other women, feel overanxious in the presence of men, and sell myself short by adjusting my behavior to fit in. All of this is running parallel to and separate from the professional successes I have enjoyed over the years. One of the joys, and there are not too many, of being an older woman is you come into your own and find your center. You discover you have found your voice and are less afraid. In fact, you might even wonder in amazement where that voice came from and ask where it has been hiding all of these years. It is not all fun as finding your voice often means you have stopped incessantly smiling or flirting to keep people happy, but that is a story for my next book. You begin to enjoy colleagueship with other women and men in ways you could not allow yourself to earlier in life. It is a loss, however, if we have to wait until we are in our 50s and 60s before we are set free from the shackles of these mind viruses. It is my hope that by holding this issue up to the light it will encourage us to be more thoughtful in the way we treat each other. We also could choose to become more mindful of these incessant negative messages running on the ticker tape we call our inner voice and find ways to turn down the volume.

Having become aware of the presence of stereotype threat you can opt to learn more about it, to become a stronger advocate for inclusion by fostering inter-group conversations across differences, and you can ensure you provide critical as well as positive/affirming feedback that would help mitigate against the tendency to confirm the feeling of being "less than," thus enhancing and bolstering feelings of inclusion. Be slow to judgment and at least entertain the possibility that there is more to the story than meets the eye. We are all entangled in a complicated web of internalized oppression. We are often taking on unavoidable negative messages about ourselves and our group to such an extent that it colors our view and impacts our behavior. First, and most importantly, we need to commit to learning more about "stereotype threat."

We need to educate ourselves on how this phenomenon shows up in relationships. Second, it is important to recognize stereotype threat does not show up *only* in relationship to dominant culture groups; it shows up within and across *all* cultural or gender based groups—men, women, People of color, LGBTI, and so on. We can all find ourselves caught in this spider's web. Third, in the absence of this knowledge and conceptual awareness, it is too easy to dismiss people as causing their own ineptitudes and incompetence, without realizing the underlying pathologies that may be the driving force. We can also provide positive role models and be advocates and allies across differences. And last, but not least, just because these pathologies exist is not a reason to explain them away and rest on our laurels, it is mission-critical for each individual and diverse group to become more aware and do their part to defang the snake and disempower the phenomenon, rather than colluding in disempowering ourselves and each other.

References

Aronson, J., M.J. Lustina, C. Good, K. Keough, C.M. Steele, and J. Brown. 1999. "Reducing Stereotype Threat." www.reducingstereotypethreat.org/bibliography_aronson_lustina_good_keough_steele_brown.html

Clark, K. 2016. "Stereotypes and the Clark Doll Test." https://explorable.com/stereotypes

Edney, H.T. 2006. "New (Clark) 'Doll Test' Produces Ugly Results." http://tinyurl.com/ybqsxug

Goldin, C., and C. Rouse. 2000. "Orchestrating Impartiality: The Impact of 'Blind' Auditions on Female Muscians." *American Economic Review* 90, no. 4, pp. 715–41.

Maass, A., C. D'Ettole, and M. Cadinu. 2008. "Checkmate? The Role of Gender Stereo Types in the Ultimate Intellectual Sport." *European Journal of Social Psychology* 38, no. 2 pp. 231–45.

Spencer, S.J., C.M. Steele, and D.M. Quinn. 1999. "Stereotype Threat and Women's Math Performance." *Journal of Experimental Social Psychology* 35, no. 1, pp. 4–28.

Steele, C.M. 2010. *Whistling Vivaldi: How Stereotypes Affect Us and What We Can Do.* New York: W. W. Norton and Company.

receiving honest feedback. Does political correctness build lack of trust because avoidance is palpable and lies in the middle of our relationships, like an elephant in the room?

Political correctness came about initially because of sexual harassment training in particular and diversity training in general. People learned directly and indirectly that it was not OK to use derogatory language, insulting labels, and inappropriate comments when discussing people of difference; it was not acceptable to make sexist or racist comments. For the most part, political correctness was effective in stopping the stream of inappropriate behaviors and comments, which any civilized person recognized as unacceptable. However, it actually had wider ramifications as it moved our relationships across difference to a buttoned-up place. We went from a Wild West, anything goes culture to a Prime of Miss Jean Brodie culture, where no one felt able to be authentic.

Male managers told me in recent years that they were not willing to close their office door when they gave a woman feedback for fear of being accused of sexual harassment. People talked about not inviting someone of the opposite gender to a business lunch for fear of having it misinterpreted. Clients told me they could not give feedback to a Person of Color for fear of being accused of being racist and People of Color told me about not getting a performance evaluation for years because they knew their boss did not want to address the issues and risk being accused of being racist. During one of my consulting projects, I was asked to review the company performance evaluation process looking for bias; I was provided with a list of the demographics of the individuals by gender and race. I had not met the candidates, but was provided with a list of their names, gender, and racial identity. In my final report, I identified one White woman whom the leaders seemed reluctant to talk about. I mentioned I knew something was not quite right with that picture; it was incongruent with their ability to provide others with feedback. My radar told me they were holding back, but based on the evidence I was given, I could not figure out the reason. When I discussed the report with the client later, I mentioned this to her and she went quiet for a few seconds and then said, "well, actually, the person you mention insists on being identified as a White woman, but she is actually a Black woman and no one wants to give her feedback."

Does it hinder or hurt our relationships when we avoid and filter what we say through the web of politeness? Are we actually just hiding our isms (racism, sexism, and so on) under a blanket of political correctness? If you had a choice, where would you want it to stop—being politically correct? Anything goes? Or somewhere in the middle? I am opting for the middle. Allow me to explain why.

The Train Has Left the Station—Next Stop "Civility"

The PC train has left the station and where it stops will inevitably determine a new "center." Political correctness is the tendency to speak with diplomacy and tact while actually covering up what you are really thinking for fear of being misunderstood. I have been on a pendulum ride with political correctness for 30+ years. When it first showed up, I believed it was a good thing and necessary to bring more civility to the conversation about difference. In recent years, I began to see evidence suggesting we had swung the pendulum too far. Being politically correct was stopping us from having courageous conversations across differences and de facto stifling relationships. However, listening with some degree of incredulity to the rhetoric surrounding the 2016 U.S. Presidential campaign has renewed my respect for political correctness. Some things are better not said.

If someone tells you they know they need to lose 40 lbs. and your response is "No, you need to lose 80 lbs." did they say that because they thought shock and awe would be helpful or did they drop all pretense at being politically correct and not care about the impact on the person? Where we draw the line and what we can do about it is an evolving story and an unfinished symphony. We may have swung the pendulum too far by becoming so PC that it has filtered our words and silenced our truths and on the other end of the continuum giving permission for people to come out swinging with no holds barred. Neither position is very effective.

Polite Consideration—An Alternative or a Cop Out

Political correctness must be approached carefully and with great attention to where the boundaries lie. We should not abandon it as it serves a very useful purpose in a civilized society. The middle of the road may seem dangerous if you are facing oncoming traffic, but moderation has power; moderation allows us to hear each other—it rebuilds the bridge to a future where relationships across differences can be courteous and diverse views and stories can be heard in an open and respectful manner. The fence is a valid position, and our goal should be to have the pendulum swing gently back to the middle. If we agree to return to civility—not "anything goes" and not "avoidance," are we able to pull it off or would that just be another name for avoidance?

PC Redefined—A New Vision

Pragmatically speaking, peaceful coexistence may be the best we can hope for, both at work and in society at large, but the extreme ends of the PC continuum will not get us there. Having given this much thought, I propose we redefine PC. I visualize a future where being "politely considerate" (as distinct from being politically correct) coupled with genuine and respectful curiosity to learn about differences allow us to be more authentic. We need to be less afraid, more courageous, and make space for each other's voices and stories. We need to work toward respecting our differences, without feeling threatened by them. However, as I write this chapter, the pendulum is still in motion. Where are you placing your vote? Are you in favor of option 1—"*Bombastic City*" where being offensive or extemporaneously outrageous is sanctioned or for option 2—"*Vanilla City*" at the buttoned-up end where we suppress and avoid, or for option 3—"*Polite Consideration*" in the middle, where we can at least talk across differences and learn to be respectful, curious, and authentic? Where do you want the pendulum to stop? What is best for you, for your organization, and long term, what is best for the continued existence of our civilized society?

CHAPTER 13

Golf, Inclusion, and the Rubik's Cube

Mark Twain is often attributed with saying, golf is a good walk spoiled.

If you never played golf, you may think golf looks easy and perhaps, even boring. But, you don't know what you don't know. If you actually tried hitting a golf ball, you would quickly realize how difficult it is to hit that little ball long, straight, *and* in the direction of the target. If you took up golf, you would discover that the more you play, the more you realize how challenging golf really is. There are very few days on the golf course where everything goes smoothly. Some days your swing plane is out of alignment and other days your head is just not in the game. In fact, when both things happen on the same day, and they do, you may want to throw your clubs in the nearest lake or bend your driver around a tree. But, during every 18 holes, you will probably hit at least one shot so amazing that it will soar through the air like your soul on wings and the allure of perfection will bring you back for another round. When you relax and swing easy, the ball goes further and your body thanks you. But golf is as much mental as it is physical and as you strive for that seductive perfect round, you will viscerally begin to understand why Arnold Palmer said the longest distance in golf is the five inches between your ears. It seems, the harder you try, the more your inner voice gets in the way; the more your body tenses up and things go awry. It is unequivocally true, the more you engage with the game, the more you will be obliged to change your initial perspective from being a passive observer who thought it was "easy" to being a player with a new respect and love for the beautiful and yet frustrating complexity. You will find yourself becoming a life-long learner in search of excellence, looking for that close-to-perfect round that can tell your grandchildren about.

But what does golf have to do with inclusion? There are many parallels on the journey to inclusion. Just like Mark Twain, we may think that spending time and effort on inclusion is not the best use of our time; after all, it is not really a business issue; it is an HR-driven program designed to take you away from your real work. We may even think inclusion is so easy that it does not require effort. But, the more we work with it, the more we are obliged to realize how complex and challenging it really is. And just like golf, when we stop being a passive observer and step into the inclusion arena, we realize it takes dedication, commitment, and practice. There will be good days and bad days. Days when we feel we are making progress and days when we want to give up. In the quest for perfection in golf, we often find ourselves in the water, in sand traps, and in the rough along the way; not quite sure how we got there and blaming our clubs or the wind or the weather or the bug that flew across our face just as we took a swing. But it never stops us coming back for more, and the same should be true for inclusion.

The Synthesizing Power of Immutable and Permeable Forces

You cannot change what you cannot see. The overarching goal of this book has been to bring recognition to the fact that the three immutable and four permeable forces discussed in previous chapters not only exist separately and synergistically, but can also be mastered if we take the time and effort required to understand them. It will not necessarily be easy, but if you stay in the game, you will get better. Inclusion is not a smooth stroll along the fairway; it is just like 18 holes of golf, full of excitement and rewards hand-in-hand with disappointments and challenges wrapped up in the immutable and permeable forces of inclusion (Figure 13.1).

Looking at the immutable forces again, if we understand *dominance* is here to stay we can, if we are willing, work to minimize its negative impact to be more inclusive. If we accept *unconscious bias* is not going away, we can work to become more cognizant of how it shows up in many forms and work to limit its power over us. If we understand there are *degrees of difference* within every diverse group, we can have much more clarity on

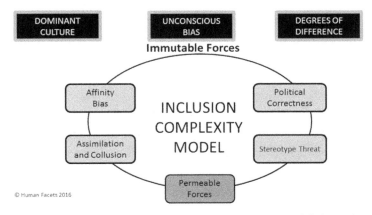

Figure 13.1 Human Facets: Inclusion complexity model (2016)

the struggle between individuality and group, and we can approach each diverse group recognizing that the differences within each group matter and must be addressed.

If we in turn understand the permeable forces of *affinity bias, assimilation, stereotype threat,* and *political correctness* are all reactions to the presence of the immutable forces, we can choose to make mid-course corrections and discuss them in a mature manner, looking to work together to minimize their impact or render them extinct.

From Unconscious Incompetence to Unconscious Competence

As I contemplate how to solve the complexity of inclusion and gain mastery over the combined forces of the three immutable forces and the four permeable forces of inclusion, I am reminded of the four levels of the *Unconscious Incompetence* model.

Level 1: Unconscious incompetence

Level 2: Conscious incompetence

Level 3: Conscious competence

Level 4: Unconscious competence

We can easily live in a state of unconscious incompetence on inclusion, where we don't know what we don't know; thinking there is really nothing to this "inclusion thing" and wondering why we need to keep talking about diversity and inclusion. I have had conversations with people who expressed the view, one day we will be able to "stop talking about this stuff." They believe it is just the "program du jour" and an HR-driven phenomenon. They are convinced if they keep their heads down long enough, it will go away and we will be on to the next best thing. They contend once we figure out how to just treat each other as human beings, we can stop discussing "it." But, nothing could be further from the truth.

Unfortunately, we cannot take a quantum leap from Level 1 or even Level 2 to Level 4, just as you cannot go on the driving range for the first time and then win the Masters a few weeks later. To excel at anything requires commitment, dedication, and practice, practice, practice. To be a professional golfer, you must understand many aspects of golf, including the geometry of the game, reading distances to the pin, factoring wind direction, aerodynamics of the swing, and the ability to read angles on the green before you putt. The same is true for inclusion.

Once we are made aware of the business case and need for action, we move from Level 1: *unconscious incompetence* where we do not even realize there is a problem to Level 2: *conscious incompetence* where we begin to realize other people may indeed have a different experience and perception/story than the one we carry, and yet, it is still not clear what the best course of action might be. This leaves us searching for answers and solutions, and generally results in leaders directing HR to set up Diversity and Inclusion programs to train employees and engage them in the inclusion conversation.

Level 3, *conscious competence*, is where we commit to engage in discussions across differences, looking to improving relationships and results. Level 3 is precisely where most corporations who conduct any kind of Diversity and Inclusion training and programs are functioning. They have seen the problem and begun to address it. The overarching reality, however, is most companies are stuck in Level 3 and unable to move to Level 4 precisely because of the tensile and combined strength of the three immutable forces and four permeable forces.

A considerable amount of money and effort has been directed toward diversity and inclusion, and over the years, we have moved from race and gender awareness training to unconscious bias and now inclusion, but we have not yet arrived. We are still spinning our wheels spending time and money hoping to graduate to Level 4. We continue the search for the Holy Grail by coming up with the next program du jour, which in turn goes viral and the cycle continues. The next initiative may well include establishing employee resource groups and training programs for White males and other members of dominant cultures to bring them back into the fold and then again it might be something we have not yet envisioned.

When we arrive at Level 4, unconscious competence, we can be inclusive without having to try too hard; where it comes naturally and we are more comfortable with difference. We will stop saying we do not notice difference. We will stop saying differences do not matter. We will not act as if we did not hear your story. Or interrupt you to tell you that "that happens to me too, so it cannot be (racism)." We will embrace differences and cease to fear them. We will respect differences and see all diverse groups well-represented at all levels of the organization. We will redefine the boundaries and create a new work space together, where we can feel safe to bring our best selves to work. We will create an environment where we can invent new and exciting products by using *all* of our collective and diverse ideas and resources. Nirvana? Maybe, but as Phillip Stanhope, 4th Earl of Chesterfield once said, "Anything worth doing is worth doing well." And to draw on my cultural roots for a moment, folklore has it that when King Robert, the Bruce of Scotland, was hiding in a cave to escape the English army, he was watching a spider trying to weave a web across the opening of the cave. According to legend, the spider tried seven times before it succeeded in reaching the other side to attach its web. As a result of the spider's tenacious determination, every child in Scotland knows that the King told his troops prior to the Battle of Hastings "If at first you don't succeed, try, try, and try again."

To follow the King's lead, or perhaps, it is the spider's lead, we must keep trying to achieve inclusion. We need to unpack the many variables and begin to build our skill set and competence across many levels. No matter what programs and initiatives you have in place and/or plan to put in place, you must ensure you take a matrix approach that addresses all three immutable forces and the four permeable forces.

You need to approach this across the vertical and horizontal axes described in Chapter 6 and also ensure all the key influencers and leadership groups are doing the same work. The following two charts provide a checklist for your strategic approach. I suggest you conduct a D & I audit and ask yourself how each of these issues is being addressed, and if not, why not? What can you put in place to ensure these conversations are happening?

✓ Completed or working on it	X not on the radar	? Not sure where to start

Immutable force	Gender	Race and culture	Sexual orientation	Other diverse group(s)
Dominance				
Unconscious bias				
Degrees of difference				
Permeable force	**Gender**	**Race and culture**	**Sexual orientation**	**Other diverse group(s)**
Affinity bias				
Assimilation bias				
Stereotype threat				
Political correctness				

Additionally, the same logic and approach must be applied (first) to the organizational levels, where key players are most likely to be influential in causing change to happen. I am aware I am about to speak the unspoken, but just being a member of a diverse group does not make you an expert on diversity and inclusion. Just because you are an exceptional leader of the Marketing Department or the best Manufacturing Manager the company has ever known does not make you qualified to step right into the role of being an advocate or champion for your company's Diversity and Inclusion program. If, for example, you are an Asian woman or a White male who is gay, you most certainly understand the story behind your own diverse group experience; however, you may not have done your own work on all of the other diversity issues and you most certainly harbor your own unconscious biases, assimilation behaviors, and internalized oppression. If you are an exceptional leader in your organization and desire to volunteer (or be volunteered) to champion the women's Group or the LGBTI group, that does not make you an expert. Leaders are appointed to Diversity Councils all the time and then at their first few meetings look at each other and wonder what they need to do. Why are we meeting? Where shall we begin? May be we should run some focus groups or look at engagement survey results? If the agenda is driven at all, it is usually initially by having everyone look to the People of Color in the room and expect them to come up with the answers.

The Diversity Department, leadership, the Diversity Council, and ERGs should first do their own work. The work of understanding must start with you or the old adage "Physician heal thyself" or "The Cobbler's children have no shoes" will surely apply if you implement programs for your employees and give yourself an exemption from doing the work. It is OK, and in fact, preferable that the Diversity Council educate themselves first. Which one of these boxes can you check, which are you working on, and which have a question mark as you do not yet know where to begin?

✓ Completed or working on it	X not on the radar	? Not sure where to start

Immutable force	Leadership team	HR and office of diversity	Diversity Council	Employee resource groups
Dominance				
Unconscious bias				
Degrees of difference				
Permeable force	**Leadership team**	**HR and office of diversity**	**Diversity Council**	**Employee resource groups**
Affinity bias				
Assimilation bias				
Stereotype threat				
Political correctness				

Expanding your world view by understanding these three immutable forces and four permeable forces and leaning in to improve awareness and create solutions will go a long way to achieving a more inclusive work-place despite living in a wider world that today seems like it has become a mitigating force against inclusion.

If you can now see the connections between them and the impact of these seven synergistic forces, you have the power to, metaphorically speaking, go where no man or woman, has gone before. If you understand their combined power is a force to be reckoned with and apply a Lean Six Sigma mentality, I have no doubt you can not only chip away at them, but gain mastery over them.

What's in a Name? A Lot

Movements have begun with the rallying cry of a few well-chosen words and the ability to have it "go viral." Even the most difficult and most challenging changes have happened after someone came up with a great phrase that took hold; consider the following:

✓ Dare to be great (President T. Roosevelt)
✓ Your country needs you (President J. F. Kennedy)
✓ Yes, we can (President Barack Obama)
✓ Just do it (Nike)
✓ Black lives matter (Black Lives Matter movement)
✓ Don't find fault, find a remedy (Henry T. Ford)

Perhaps, Starbucks idea of writing "Race together" on your coffee cup and starting a conversation with your Barista to solve 400 years of racism while holding up the line was not the best idea, but the intent was correct. We need to talk to each other about these three immutable and four permeable forces; we need to lean in and not back off; we need to have the courage and commitment to embrace differences.

If and when we put our minds to it, we can generate a movement to become more inclusive at work, at home, and in society at large. If we can put a man on the moon, surely we can come together at work and at home to figure out inclusion. Inclusion is the only viable option. In a world of increasing divisiveness, the issue has become bigger than just the talent pipeline and retaining great talent. We need each other. We are stronger together. Together we are more capable, more productive, more creative, and more innovative. We must learn how to widen our circle of inclusion and build trust where there was none and break the silence across difference.

CHAPTER 14

Peaceful Coexistence: A Line in the Sand and a Call to Action

Buckminster Fuller said, the best way to predict the future is to design it.

The perfect ending to this book would be to paint a rosy picture about our ability to design a flawlessly inclusive workplace, but before I can go there, I need to be realistic.

We live in a VUCA world—a world of volatility, uncertainty, complexity, and ambiguity. Perhaps, the only thing we can be certain of is change and the ambiguity of how to handle it. Working with diversity and inclusion is no exception. While it would be nice to argue that things are getting easier, they seem to have become more difficult. We are living in a world with increasing tension and violence, where more people have reason to fear and hate than ever in recent history. As I write, people are marching in Pro-White rallies and opposing Anti-White groups are being arrested in a major U.S. city. It seems we are growing further apart, and conspiring forces give us more reason to fear people not like us. What is happening is affecting all of us. Corporate leaders, legal corporations, and individual employees are no exception. When we read about an act of terror and then about a young student being removed from a U.S. flight for speaking his native language to his elderly uncle, we cannot ignore what is happening outside of work. It will have an impact on our enthusiasm for difference in the workplace, not just in the United States, but globally.

It is difficult to compartmentalize our thoughts and feelings. How can we stop our anxiety from leaking over and tainting our sincere attempts to create an inclusive environment at work? How can we stop rolling our eyes or shaking our heads in quiet resignation?

However, on the upside if there is an obvious place where learning can occur and time and money *will* be invested in teaching us to be more inclusive, it is surely the corporate world. In addition to tackling inclusion to retain top talent, we have the capacity to put a realistic and definitive plan in place to make the workplace not only the nexus for increased creativity, innovation, productivity, and inclusion, but a template and a role model for how we can live together outside of work. But that does not mean it will be easy.

From Spinning Our Wheels to Gaining Traction

"Shoot for the moon and you may land on the stars" is a popular cliché, but with the magnitude of challenges we face today, a partial commitment is not enough. Before we shoot for the moon, we need to keep our feet on the ground and face the reality of what is happening. Half-hearted goals will not work and lip service to inclusion will surely maintain the status quo. We should collectively make a conscious corporate decision to rise above the fray and separate ourselves from the increasing global and societal divide. Jack Canfield said, "Everything you want is on the other side of fear" (Canfield and Hansen 2013). A future of increased fear, hatred, and separation is not where we need to arrive.

When the business world first started discussing inclusion, we focused on improving the talent pipeline and ensuring retention of top talent; we wanted to hire and promote diversity at every level in the organization. These goals remain, and in fact, are more imperative than ever, given the changing world demographics. Everything we have discussed in this book will help you address them. We now need to factor in people carry heightened anxiety about differences. If we are serious about wanting more inclusivity, we must confront these realities, step up to the challenge, and put programs in place to unite people both locally and globally.

One of the areas where we consistently fail to be inclusive is in not understanding the impact of U.S.-centric or Western European dominance in regional and geographically diverse corporate locations. Over the years, I have had many conversations with representatives from regional offices of Fortune 500 companies. Till this day, they express frustration at having their corporate offices tell them how to manage the diversity and inclusion challenges they face in their geography. To be more fully inclusive, one needs to take account of these differences and to ensure local people have a voice in developing a solution that speaks to local issues and not just to the corporate agenda. There is a move today from globalization to glocalization where expats are replaced by local leaders. However, even then, companies still impose global programs or U.S.-based programs on these local leaders. It is important to provide the flexibility to customize and/or to implement more relevant local programs that speak directly to that employee base. It is fine to recommend a corporately centered template, but necessary to ensure each region feels their voice is heard.

A Recap

Throughout this book, I have given you a lot of concepts and ideas to consider. I presented innumerable ideas and paradoxes, new ways of thinking about your own beliefs, and new insights into the beliefs of others. Just by reading this book, you have begun the journey and are much closer to understanding what it takes to be more inclusive.

You may realize you are not as unbiased as you thought and now accept you must look beyond your dominance and be willing to hear other perspectives. Perhaps, as a member of a subculture, you believed dominant culture people are deliberately holding out and now you can see we are all in this together; unconsciously colluding in a multifaceted puzzle that requires all our efforts to solve.

Perhaps, you thought just because you are "diverse" that you "get it" and reading about affinity bias, assimilation, stereotype threat, and internalized oppression made you realize *you also* have work to do. Perhaps, you feel you have done a lot of this work and you are in pretty good shape when it comes to your inclusion mindset, but have you caught any of your regressive behaviors after reading this book?

If you stayed with me through the preceding 13 chapters, it is a pretty safe bet you have covered all of the concepts and read all of my stories. But, did you notice the threats that run through these stories—of vulnerability, regression, and being allowed to be human? When you focus on these, you will realize they consistently told their own story. Those stories feed directly into the bigger picture of inclusion. It takes courage to be vulnerable, and it particularly takes courage to share stories that demonstrate our personal challenges with being inclusive. I have always found when people are willing to share real stories, I can relate to them more easily. So, I hope my ability to be authentic and share real stories has helped you to relate.

Once we realize the value of being vulnerable, what's the value of understanding regression when it comes to inclusion? We all regress; we want to put our best foot forward every time; we want people to believe we are always our best self, but we know that is simply not true. I am a diversity and inclusion expert, and yet, I am not always fully in alignment when it comes to valuing differences. We are not perfect human beings and no one will graduate with an A+ from Inclusion University. We are all humans and I advocate in addition to launching new business initiatives to address the three immutable forces and four permeable forces you allow for vulnerability and evidence of regression in yourself and others; that you understand there will be times when people are not perfectly aligned with inclusion, and we are all, after all, humans. However, this is not a reason to abdicate responsibility for inclusion; it is merely an attempt to be realistic about our human frailties. I do have some final suggestions for you to work on as individuals as you strive to overcome those frailties.

From Corporate Programs to Individual Actions

In Chapter 13, I suggested a plan for corporations and their leaders and employees to address the immutable and permeable forces and encourage systemic change. In this final chapter, I offer you a few ideas on how you as an individual can become an effective change agent for inclusion.

Using yourself as an instrument of change is not new and is an important concept when we look at diversity and inclusion. It is certainly an indisputable truth, we are all individuals and as such have choices, particularly about use of self. When it comes to being an individual, there are certain things you can do to ensure you are a proactive champion for inclusion at work.

Use Yourself as an Inclusion Change Agent

The late Dr. Charlie Seashore was one of my mentors. I first met Charlie at the National Training Laboratories in Bethel, Maine. I selected my PhD program at Fielding based on knowing he was on the faculty. He, along with his late wife, Edie, was an internationally renowned expert on *Use of Self*. The Seashore Model for use of self includes agency, giving and receiving feedback, reframing, self-efficacy, skills, and support systems (Seashore 2001; Seashore et al. 2004). His way of working with others and influence on me was the cornerstone for my journey into self-reflection and inclusion. Out of deep respect for his memory, I created a roadmap of inclusion skills by adapting the six attributes of intentional use of self as my guide. If you use these attributes for your inclusion journey, they will help you be more conscious of each step you must take to not only build skills but improve relationships:

1. *Agency and inclusion*: Taking responsibility to act on your own initiative in exploring your inclusion journey.
2. *Giving and receiving feedback and inclusion*: Continual willingness toward self-reflection and the courage to invite regular feedback from key "others" who can provide insights into how you are doing and tell you what you still need to learn and improve. Key others should include people from your own diverse groups and individuals from other diverse groups to ensure a cross section of perceptions. This feedback should be regular and you should consider asking a couple of people to be your mentors; to hold you accountable and tell you when they see improvements or notice you are slipping on your agreed behavior changes.
3. *Reframing and inclusion*: When you receive new information about inclusion, or have light bulb moments, having the ability and willingness to reframe your experiences, mental models, and stories. This requires an ability to add the new information to your library of inclusion skills and knowledge, and not just discard it as a one-off-learning experience.

4. *Self-Efficacy and inclusion*: A belief in your capacity to achieve a more inclusive work environment in your immediate surroundings and to become a more sensitive, curious, and inclusive individual.

5. *Skills for inclusion*: Dr. Charlie talked about this category as the need to learn more about communication, listening, goal-setting, conflict management, team building, and maintaining effective relationships along with stress management. One of my online assessment tools, the Inclusion Skills Measurement Profile (ISM Profile), which measures inclusion skills use seven skills categories that closely match these attributes. The ISM Profile skill categories are—Diversity Sensitivity, Integrity with Difference, Interacting with Difference, Valuing Difference, Team Inclusion; Resolving Conflict across Difference and Embedding Inclusion. Skills gaps in any of these categories can get in the way of us being inclusive and form significant blind spots. Here is a table of the key competencies needed to ensure you build individual proficiency as an inclusion champion.

Inclusion Skills Category	Key competency questions
Diversity Sensitivity: Become more aware of difference and gain a higher level of self-awareness	Do you monitor own diversity sensitivity and impact on others? Do you make a conscious effort to learn about those who are different? Are you proactive in exposing yourself to a range of experiences with those who are different? Do you continually take steps to improve your own diversity awareness?
Integrity with Difference: Honor the differences of your own social identity group(s)	Are you aware of your personal attitudes and beliefs about members of own social identity group? Are you vigilant about the tendency to discount yourself and members of your own social identity group due to the negative messages surrounding internalized oppression?
	Do you encourage people from your own social identity group(s) to acknowledge and own the merits of their difference, while honoring the diversity in others?

Interacting with Difference: Demonstrates high level of interpersonal skills when interacting with people from diverse backgrounds	Do you listen actively for other frames of reference without prejudging? Do you seek to understand and adapt to different styles? Do you treat others as they wish to be treated? Do you show willingness to change the way you do things to meet the needs of those from diverse backgrounds?
Valuing Difference: Treat diversity as an asset	Do you encourage innovation and creativity in the workplace? Do you embrace diversity as a resource to benefit the organization and its members? Do you ensure there are supports systems, procedures, and practices in place that promote diversity in the workforce? Do you look for opportunities to leverage the benefits differences can add?
Team Inclusion	Do you take every opportunity to ensure that project teams and work groups are diverse? Do you encourage and capitalize on the diverse contributions and strengths of team members? Do you practice inclusive behaviors in groups and intervene sensitively when exclusionary behaviors occur?
Resolving conflict over Difference: Recognize and respect different styles of conflict resolution	Do you make a conscious effort to learn about different styles of conflict resolution? Do you have insights into your own preferred conflict management style and its impact on others? Do you flex your conflict style to accommodate others? Are you proactive in resolving conflict over difference when it arises, or are you more comfortable avoiding it?
	Do you actively create the space for people to use different forms of conflict resolution when conflict occurs?

(Continued)

(Continued)

Embedding Inclusion:	Are you actively involved with organizational issues that promote diversity awareness?
Advocate for inclusion within your sphere of influence—at work and within the wider community	Do you constantly seek out opportunities to lobby influential individuals and groups on issues of diversity and inclusion?
	Do you challenge prejudice and injustice, when confronted with evidence of it in the workplace, directly or indirectly?
	Are you an active advocate of treating people fairly and accommodating difference in all spheres of life, that is, personal, social, and professional, and within the wider community?

6. *Support systems for inclusion*: It is perhaps a no-brainer that to be successful at inclusion, you have to be inclusive of others. In order to do that, you need to build support systems around you. It is important as you continue this journey to build support networks of people you trust, people who are willing to be honest with you, people you can talk to about your questions and concerns, and people who are in your corner on good and bad days. It goes without saying that this network should include people from your own diverse groups and from other diverse groups.

A Game Changer: Leading the Way

If your company's Diversity and Inclusion program previously had you rolling your eyes and saying, "Why do I need to do this? Or "I wish it would just go away," then I hope this book helped you answer that question and work through your frustration. Having a negative attitude toward inclusion is one of the biggest stumbling blocks. But, if you can move beyond that obstacle and are willing to not only start the process, but also to stay the course you, will make a difference, not just to the quality of your individual lives, but also to the quality of relationships in the workplace and in society. My hope is what you have read here and learned have already changed you and opened your mind to a new and more hopeful perspective on the diversity and inclusion story. I have confidence it made you a more curious learner; willing to lean in and learn more.

The Complete Picture

If you implement the suggestions in this book, you will find yourself standing on the precipice of Level 4 on the road to becoming "unconsciously competent" (Figure 14.1).

I started the book talking about the complexity of inclusion and want to wrap up by reinforcing the Inclusion Complexity model. Here is where it all comes together. The three immutable forces (Dominance, Unconscious Bias, and Degrees of Difference) and the four permeable forces (Affinity Bias, Assimilation Bias, Political Correctness, and Stereotype threat/internalized oppression). They are all interconnected and operating simultaneously. If we can keep our eyes on the model, it will allow us to see the big picture. We can unpack its component parts at an individual and collective level and discover we have the roadmap to success.

A Quantum Leap: From Business to Society?

Imagine we have become masters at managing inclusion, and our corporate programs are on an accelerated pathway to success, a success that

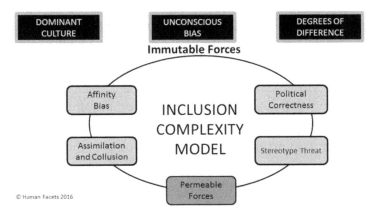

Figure 14.1 Human Facets: Inclusion complexity model (2016)

breaks glass ceilings and retains top talent at all levels. Great job, congratulations! But knowing we are overachievers and always looking for the next great project, where do we go from here? What are we capable of once we overcome our resistance to inclusion and subdue our self-induced natural tendencies to resist differences? I have a somewhat unconventional suggestion.

It is not unconventional to acknowledge people learn things at work they can and do apply at home. But what is unconventional is the idea of asking the corporate world to accept a bigger responsibility to embrace not only inclusion at work, but the societal need for more inclusion as part of their corporate social responsibility program (CSR). If Richard Branson can think outside of the box and envision Virgin Galactic and the creation of the first commercially viable suborbital flight into space, then the sky really is the limit.

There is no question that learned inclusion skills and concepts are directly transferrable to our relationships outside of work. They are fundamental to human nature and go to the core of who we are and how we behave. When we can grasp them, we can not only help to improve the workplace, we can also make business and society better.

When we can make these changes, we will move from spinning our wheels around the inclusion axis to gaining traction on inclusion. We will shift the conversation and awareness toward bringing people closer to an understanding of how to capitalize on our differences—a desired state where everyone wins. If we succeed in doing that, then it is not beyond the realms of possibility that building more conscious awareness and inclusion skills at work can have a transformational effect on relationships outside of work. In the movie "Peter Pan," Peter tells Wendy at the end of the movie:

> "You know that place between sleep and awake? The place where you can still remember dreaming? That's where I will always love you. That's where I will be waiting." *Peter Pan*

The very idea we could leverage our corporate agenda on inclusion and turn it into a much bigger initiative may seem like a fantasy or overly ambitious, like living in that place between sleep and awake, but if not us, then who? If not now, then when? I spoke with an HR employee recently who said seeing the company's diversity and inclusion agenda as having a bigger purpose was very motivating and exciting. What about you? In your opinion, is inclusion related only to the bottom line or could it grow in importance and be part of the CSR program? Could you see it as having a bigger purpose that would give it a wider reach? If corporations, as legal citizens, are willing to do their part to fight climate change and implement recycling programs, then why not create a movement for inclusion? The good news is we know we have already begun the journey, and on the way, we can hope to create a positive tipping point and become the driving force for a game changer of peaceful coexistence.

It is often said that we teach what we want to learn. Throughout the book I have shared stories from my own personal and professional journey with inclusion. As I wind up this last chapter and I reflect on my experiences with the "illusion of inclusion," I realize there have been times over the years when I have tried too hard to be included or liked, both within and across diverse groups. I have trusted where no trust was merited or earned, and I have given people a second and third chance only to discover the noise of my desire to be included drowned out the warning signs and red flags. I trusted people professionally and personally who were not worthy of my trust, people who were not honorable about their reasons for including me. These experiences leave scars and could make it easy for me to justify giving up on inclusion, but I consciously choose not to do that, preferring instead to let inclusion win.

Call to Action: #letinclusionwin

Reading this book and implementing the suggestions contained within these three immutable forces and four permeable forces will be a game changer, not just for the workplace, but for society at large. The corporate world could lead the way by making a significant contribution toward a more cohesive society; a society with less hatred, more acceptance, and more understanding. I don't know about you, but that thought makes me excited enough to get out of bed in the morning and keep putting on my inclusion cape. What about you? Are you willing to rise to the challenge and #letinclusionwin?

References

Canfield, J., and M.V. Hansen. 2013. *Chicken Soup for the Soul.* Chicken Soup for the Soul Publishing.

Seashore, C. 2001. "Reframing—Increasing One's Power Through Mental Gymnastics." Organization Development Network, New York.

Seashore, C.N., M.N. Shawver, G. Thompson, and M. Mattare. 2004. "Doing Good by Knowing Who You Are: The Instrumental Self as an Agent of Change." *OD Practitioner* 36, no. 3, pp. 42–46.

Index

OTHER TITLES IN THE HUMAN RESOURCE MANAGEMENT AND ORGANIZATIONAL BEHAVIOR COLLECTION

- *Major in Happiness: Debunking the College Major Fallacies* by Michael Edmondson
- *The Resilience Advantage: Stop Managing Stress and Find Your Resilience* by Richard S. Citrin and Alan Weiss
- *Success: Theory and Practice* by Michael Edmondson
- *Manage Your Career: 10 Keys to Survival and Success When Interviewing and on the Job, Second Edition* by Vijay Sathe
- *The New Leader: Harnessing the Power of Creativity to Produce Change* by Renee Kosiarek
- *Performance Leadership* by Karen Moustafa Leonard and Fatma Pakdil
- *You're a Genius: Using Reflective Practice to Master the Craft of Leadership* by Steven S. Taylor
- *Leading the Positive Organization: Actions, Tools, and Processes* by Thomas N. Duening, et al

Announcing the Business Expert Press Digital Library

Concise e-books business students need for classroom and research

This book can also be purchased in an e-book collection by your library as

- a one-time purchase,
- that is owned forever,
- allows for simultaneous readers,
- has no restrictions on printing, and
- can be downloaded as PDFs from within the library community.

Our digital library collections are a great solution to beat the rising cost of textbooks. E-books can be loaded into their course management systems or onto students' e-book readers.
The **Business Expert Press** digital libraries are very affordable, with no obligation to buy in future years. For more information, please visit **www.businessexpertpress.com/librarians**. To set up a trial in the United States, please email **sales@businessexpertpress.com**.

CPSIA information can be obtained
at www.ICGtesting.com
Printed in the USA
LVHW02s1921300418
575428LV00007B/37/P